worm composting made easy

DIY Vermiculture, Waste Management, Compost
Bins, Earthworm Care, and Soil Enrichment

Sustainable Living and Gardening
Book Five

harper wells

life level up books, llc.

Worm Composting Made Easy: DIY Vermiculture, Waste Management, Compost Bins, Earthworm Care, and Soil Enrichment

Copyright © 2023 by Harper Wells

contents

introduction

. . .

IN THE EVER-EVOLVING tapestry of our world, where the threads of sustainability and ecological responsibility are intricately woven, a movement is taking root—a revolution of the smallest but mightiest creatures—the earthworms. These humble beings, with their miraculous abilities to transform organic waste into black gold, hold the key to a greener, more sustainable future. Experience the fascinating realm of vermicomposting, waste management, compost bins, earthworm care, and soil enrichment.

A BUSTLING METROPOLIS, an idyllic countryside, or even a humble urban backyard—their common thread is the generation of organic waste. The discarded remains of fruits, vegetables, and other kitchen scraps pile up, often destined for landfills, where their decomposition contributes to harmful greenhouse gases. But here's where our heroes come into play—the earthworms, nature's industrious recyclers, the unsung heroes of sustainable waste management.

THIS BOOK IS NOT JUST a mere guide; it's an invitation to partake in a powerful mission—a mission to redefine our relationship

1

with waste, to transform it from a burden into a resource, and to embrace a circular economy through the magic of vermicomposting.

IN THE FIRST chapter of our expedition, we dive into the very core of vermicomposting's significance. Let's understand the profound environmental impact of organic waste and explore the plethora of benefits that come with composting alongside our wriggly allies. From enriching soil to reducing our carbon footprint, vermicomposting is a beacon of hope, shining a light on the path to a more sustainable tomorrow.

VENTURING DEEPER, we get to know our earthworm companions, unraveling the secrets of their role in soil health and uncovering the diverse array of composting and earthworm species. And let us not forget the delightful intricacies of their anatomy and behavior—tales of locomotion through the soil, their voracious appetites for organic matter, and their tireless efforts in soil aeration and nutrient enrichment.

WE'VE REACHED a fork in the road as we put up our vermicomposting systems. It is critical to choose the best place for our composting efforts, as well as to select and prepare the ideal compost bin or container. Fear not, for within these pages, we will equip you with the knowledge to create an optimal environment for your earthworm allies to thrive.

AS WE VENTURE into the heart of our vermicomposting odyssey, we discover the importance of bedding and the art of preparing a nurturing habitat for our earthworm friends. The magic of moisture and aeration unfolds before us, revealing the secrets to maintaining a balanced and thriving vermicomposting bed.

. . .

NEXT, we take a closer look at selecting and introducing the perfect earthworm companions for our vermicomposting. Just as in any community, compatibility is key, and we dive into the characteristics of suitable earthworm species while learning how to acclimate them to their new home.

FEEDING our earthworm allies is an art form, as we identify appropriate food sources and establish a feeding routine for efficient composting. Join us in this gastronomic adventure, while we navigate common feeding mistakes and ensure our worm companions dine like royalty.

WITH A WELL-FED and contented worm community, we turn our attention to their care and maintenance. The balance of moisture becomes paramount as we explore strategies to assess and regulate the moisture requirements of our vermicomposting systems. In tandem, we embrace the power of temperature control and learn how external factors can influence our worm's activity and reproductive success.

ALAS, even in this Eden of composting, challenges can arise. Pests may encroach upon our vermicomposting sanctuaries. Fret not! We shall uncover the secrets of pest management, employing safe and effective methods to protect our worms without resorting to harmful measures.

LET'S discover an abundance of composting materials and food sources to fuel our vermicomposting endeavors. From kitchen scraps to garden clippings, we explore a vast array of organic waste, understanding the carbon-to-nitrogen ratio and its significance. With this knowledge, we categorize materials into greens, browns, and other compostable items, laying the groundwork for nutrient-rich vermicompost.

. . .

JOIN us as we unlock the secrets of harvesting vermicompost, utilizing it to nurture gardens and landscapes, and even exploring innovative applications of vermiculture in diverse fields.

So, whether you're a seasoned vermicomposter or a curious novice, this book is your gateway to a world of environmental stewardship and the joy of composting with our wriggly co-inhabitants. As we embark together on this remarkable adventure, let us unite as a community of eco-warriors, spreading the worm composting movement and inspiring others to embrace the transformative power of vermicomposting.

COME, let us dive headfirst into the world of "Worm Composting Made Easy," where hope, encouragement, and actionable advice await you at every turn. The revolution starts now, and it starts with you. Get ready to the future—a future where earthworms and humans collaborate to create a greener, more sustainable planet.

worm composting

. . .

Unleashing Nature's Tiny Recycling Heroes

IT'S time to bid farewell to the traditional compost heap and say hello to a sustainable, eco-friendly solution that's as fascinating as it is beneficial. Get ready to meet your new composting allies, the mighty earthworms!

YOU MIGHT BE WONDERING, "Why on earth should I get excited about composting with worms?" Well, dear reader, aside from the undeniable cool factor of nurturing an army of composting superheroes, worm composting offers an array of practical benefits that will rock your sustainable socks off.

SUSTAINABILITY REINVENTED: In a world grappling with environmental challenges, worm composting is a small but impactful step towards a greener future. By diverting organic waste from landfills, you're reducing harmful methane emissions while producing nutrient-rich compost that nourishes the soil and promotes healthy plant growth.

SPACE-SAVVY SOLUTION: Living in a tiny urban apartment with barely enough room to swing a cat? Fear not! Worm bins are compact and can fit comfortably on your balcony or even under the kitchen sink. You don't need a sprawling garden to do your part in sustainability; a bit of floor space will do!

Low-Maintenance Companions: Let's face it; not all of us were born with green thumbs. The beauty of worm composting lies in its simplicity. These soil-dwelling invertebrates are remarkably low-maintenance. With a bit of love and some kitchen scraps, they'll merrily chomp away, turning your waste into rich compost without demanding much attention.

Supercharged Soil: Forget store-bought fertilizers laden with chemicals. Worm castings, or worm poop (yes, you heard that right), are a nutrient-packed, all-natural fertilizer that invigorates your plants, boosts their resilience, and wards off pesky pests.

Now that you're sufficiently excited about the prospect of turning your kitchen scraps into black gold, let's dive into the nitty-gritty of worm composting.

First things first - worm species matter! Not all worms are cut out for composting duties. The real composting champs are red wigglers (Eisenia fetida) and their close relatives, the European nightcrawlers (Eisenia hortensis). These speedy composters are voracious eaters, devouring up to half their weight in organic matter every day. Talk about being the MVPs of composting!

Next up, you'll need a cozy home for your wormy buddies. Enter the worm bin! You can either purchase a ready-made worm bin or flex your DIY muscles and craft one from repurposed materials. Remember to drill some ventilation holes because even worms need fresh air!

. . .

ONCE YOUR WORM bin is set up and the worms have moved in, it's time to feed them. But what do worms eat, you ask? Almost anything organic! Fruit and veggie scraps, coffee grounds, tea bags, eggshells, and even shredded paper or cardboard - worms are equal opportunity eaters. However, steer clear of meat, dairy, and oily foods, as they can cause a stinky mess and attract unwanted guests.

AH, the magic of the feedback loop! As your wormy pals munch through the kitchen scraps, they leave behind nutrient-rich castings. Mix this black gold into your garden soil or sprinkle it on your potted plants, and watch them thrive like never before. It's like a never-ending cycle of nourishment!

IN THE WORLD of worm composting, you'll inevitably face some challenges. Temperature, moisture, and bedding conditions require a bit of attention, but don't fret - with a little observation and adjustment, you'll be a composting maestro in no time.

So, dear reader, embark on this composting adventure with an open mind, a willing heart, and a newfound appreciation for the wonders of nature's recycling system. Worm composting isn't just about converting waste into valuable fertilizer; it's about embracing a lifestyle that promotes balance, sustainability, and the understanding that even the smallest actions can have a big impact.

Sustainable Waste Management: Understanding the Environmental Impact of Organic Waste

ORGANIC WASTE, such as food scraps, yard trimmings, and other biodegradable materials, constitutes a significant portion of our overall waste stream. When this organic waste ends up in landfills, it decomposes without access to oxygen, leading to the production of methane—a potent greenhouse gas. Methane contributes to climate change and exacerbates global warming, making organic waste management a pressing concern.

Exploring the Benefits of Composting with Worms

Now THAT WE comprehend the environmental impact of organic waste, let's explore one fascinating and effective solution: vermicomposting, or composting with worms! Vermicomposting is a natural process in which earthworms, often red wigglers, break down organic matter into nutrient-rich compost. This sustainable method not only diverts waste from landfills but also produces a valuable resource for enriching soil fertility.

THINK about having your own worm composting bin right in your backyard, where these tiny eco-warriors tirelessly convert your kitchen scraps into black gold—a dark, crumbly compost perfect for nurturing your plants. We'll guide you through the simple steps of setting up your vermicomposting system and maintaining it effortlessly.

Promoting a Circular Economy through Vermicomposting

As WE EXPLORE VERMICOMPOSTING, we also embrace the principles of a circular economy. The concept of the circular economy revolves around minimizing waste and maximizing the value of resources by keeping them in use for as long as possible. Vermicomposting embodies this philosophy, where organic waste transforms into compost, nourishes the soil, fosters plant growth, and completes the cycle by eventually becoming food for us once more.

THE CIRCULAR ECONOMY CREATES A HARMONIOUS, regenerative loop that lessens the strain on our environment and reduces the need for harmful synthetic fertilizers. By adopting vermicomposting, we take a giant leap towards building a more sustainable, resilient future for generations to come.

THROUGHOUT THIS CHAPTER, we've uncovered the significance of sustainable waste management, specifically focusing on organic waste and vermicomposting. By implementing these eco-friendly practices, we can significantly reduce our environmental impact, combat climate change, and promote a circular economy.

AS YOU EMBRACE the power of vermicomposting, remember that each small action counts. The simple act of composting with worms can contribute to a monumental change when embraced by communities worldwide.

TOGETHER, we can turn waste into wealth and nourish not only our soil but also our souls with the satisfaction of contributing to a more sustainable world. Let's empower ourselves with knowledge and take action for a brighter future!

REMEMBER, every step you take matters. Start vermicomposting today and be part of the solution—the solution that will shape a better, more sustainable world for generations to come.

Getting to Know Earthworms: Unveiling the Role of Earthworms in Soil Health

YOU MIGHT WONDER what makes these seemingly simple creatures so important, but as we unravel the mysteries, you'll discover how they play a pivotal role in maintaining the health of our soil and ultimately, our planet. Understanding earthworms and their impact on soil health can empower you to make a positive difference in your own garden or farming practices, and contribute to the greater goal of sustainable agriculture.

UNEARTHING THE SIGNIFICANCE OF EARTHWORMS: Let's begin by understanding why earthworms are essential to soil health. Earthworms are natural ecosystem engineers, tirelessly working beneath the surface, aerating the soil, and enhancing its fertility. As they burrow through the earth, they create channels, allowing air and water to penetrate deeper, promoting better root growth for plants. Moreover, their digestive process converts organic matter into nutrient-rich castings, commonly known as worm castings or vermicompost, which serve as a natural fertilizer for the soil.

DIFFERENTIATING between Composting and Earthworm Species: Now that we've grasped the significance of earthworms, it's crucial to distinguish between the various species and understand their unique roles. There are two primary categories: composting worms and earthworms found in the soil. Composting worms, such as red wigglers (Eisenia fetida) and European nightcrawlers (Eisenia hortensis), thrive in compost bins and are excellent at breaking down kitchen scraps. On the other hand, earthworms like Lumbricus terrestris are more common in garden soils and have specialized behaviors that enhance soil structure and nutrient cycling.

EXPLORING the Anatomy and Behavior of Earthworms: To truly appreciate earthworms, we need to get up close and personal with their fascinating anatomy and behavior. From their segmented bodies and the role of the clitellum in reproduction to the way they move through the soil, each aspect of their biology contributes to their unique functions. Understanding their behavior can help us create environments that encourage their activity and further enhance soil health.

Embracing Earthworms as Soil Health Allies

Now THAT WE'VE acquired a deeper knowledge of earthworms, let's explore practical ways to embrace them as allies in our pursuit of soil health. Implementing vermiculture techniques and creating worm-friendly environments in our gardens or farms can provide a sustainable and natural boost to soil fertility. We'll discuss how to set up a worm composting system, introduce earthworms to outdoor beds, and optimize conditions to ensure their success and proliferation.

You'VE SUCCESSFULLY UNVEILED the essential role of earthworms in soil health. By understanding their significance, differentiating between species, exploring their anatomy and behavior, and embracing them as allies, you've taken the first steps toward building a healthier and more sustainable ecosystem. As you put this knowledge into action, remember that every small effort counts in nurturing our planet for future generations. Embrace the humble earthworm and be part of the movement towards a greener and more harmonious world.

Sustainable Gardening: Setting Up Your Worm Composting System

HERE's a guide on setting up your very own worm composting system, helping you take a significant step towards a more sustainable and eco-friendly lifestyle. By understanding the bene-fits of worm composting and learning how to create an ideal environment for your earthworms, you'll be well on your way to reducing waste and cultivating healthier plants.

CHOOSING the Right Location for your Composting Setup: Find a suitable spot for your worm composting system. It should be sheltered from extreme weather conditions, such as direct sunlight, heavy rain, or freezing temperatures. Consider convenience. Select a location close to your kitchen for easy access when disposing of food scraps.

SELECTING and Preparing the Compost Bin or Container: Choose a compost bin or container that suits your needs. It should be well-ventilated to allow air circulation for the worms. Drill small holes in the bin's lid and sides to facilitate air exchange while preventing any unwanted pests from entering. Line the bottom of the bin with moistened newspaper or cardboard bedding, providing a comfortable home for the worms.

CREATING an Optimal Environment for your Earthworms: Add a layer of organic matter like kitchen scraps (fruit peels, vegetable trimmings, coffee grounds) to the bedding in the bin. Avoid meat, dairy, and oily foods as they may attract pests. Introduce red wiggler worms (Eisenia fetida) to the bin. These composting champions are efficient and thrive in confined spaces. Cover the worms with more bedding and moisten it slightly to maintain the required moisture level for their well-being.

MAINTAINING YOUR WORM COMPOSTING SYSTEM: Feed your worms regularly with small amounts of kitchen scraps. Remember not to overfeed, as it may lead to odors and fruit fly problems. Ensure the bedding remains moist but not water-logged. Add water as needed to maintain the right level of moisture. Every few months, separate the finished compost from the bin using a simple harvesting method, leaving the worms in the bedding to continue their composting work.

Troubleshooting and Tips for Success

IF YOU ENCOUNTER any unpleasant smells, it might indicate overfeeding or improper ventilation. Adjust the feeding and make sure the bin has adequate airflow.

AVOID ADDING acidic food waste like citrus peels in large quantities, as it can disrupt the worms' environment. Regularly check the composting process and ensure the worms are healthy and active.

YOU'VE NOW SET up your very own worm composting system and taken a significant step towards sustainable gardening. By embracing worm composting, you're reducing waste, enriching your garden soil, and contributing to a greener planet. Remember to maintain your worm composting system with care, and soon enough, you'll witness the magic of these little garden helpers turning your kitchen scraps into black gold for your plants.

building your
vermiculture system

. . .

VERMICULTURE IS the art and science of using earthworms to decompose organic waste and transform it into nutrient-dense, garden-ready compost. Forget about the smelly, labor-intensive compost heap in your backyard; a well-managed vermiculture system is compact, efficient, and virtually odor-free! Plus, it's a win-win situation - you reduce your ecological footprint while getting a nutrient-rich fertilizer for your plants. How cool is that?

"BUT WAIT," you may ask, "aren't worms just icky crawlies that belong in the dirt?" Well, buckle up, because today we're challenging conventional wisdom. These slimy creatures may seem unremarkable, but they're the unsung heroes of soil health and waste management. Just like a rock band needs a drummer to keep the beat, a thriving ecosystem needs worms to maintain balance and harmony in the soil.

THINK about your garden as a high-end restaurant, and the worms are the talented, Michelin-starred chefs behind the scenes. They're constantly preparing a delectable feast of decomposing matter, breaking down kitchen scraps and garden waste into a nutrient-rich symphony that nourishes your plants. As if that wasn't impressive enough, they're also digging tunnels through the soil, creating a network of passageways for air and water. It's like they're building an underground highway system for plant roots! Talk about an efficient workforce.

CREATING your own vermiculture system is easier than you might think. Here's a step-by-step guide to get you started:

- Pick the Right Worms: Not all worms are created equal. For vermiculture, you need red wigglers (Eisenia fetida) or redworms (Lumbricus rubellus). These voracious eaters have an insatiable appetite for organic matter and are excellent composters.
- Choose the Right Container: You can use a store-bought worm bin or get creative and make your own using a plastic container with a lid. Just remember to drill some holes for ventilation and drainage.
- Bedding is Key: Worms need a cozy bedding to thrive. Shredded newspaper, cardboard, or coconut coir are excellent choices. Avoid using glossy paper or materials treated with chemicals - you don't want to poison your tiny composting superheroes!
- Worms Need to Eat Too: Feed your worms a balanced diet of kitchen scraps like vegetable peels, coffee grounds, and eggshells. But, hold the dairy, meat, and oily foods - worms aren't big fans of those.
- Keep It Moist: Worms breathe through their skin, so keep the bedding moist like a wrung-out sponge. Not too wet, not too dry - aim for the Goldilocks zone.
- Patience, Grasshopper: Vermiculture isn't an overnight success. It takes a few months for your worm colony to establish and start producing compost. But trust me, the wait is worth it.

Now, you might be wondering, "How does all this worm magic benefit me beyond a thriving garden?" Good question, young grasshopper. Vermiculture is a gateway to understanding nature's delicate feedback loops. Just like the worms nourish the soil, the enriched soil nourishes your plants, and your plants eventually nourish you. It's a beautiful, interconnected dance between humans, worms, and plants.

BUT LET's not get too sentimental here. Vermiculture is also about efficiency and resourcefulness. It's about reducing waste and turning something most people toss in the trash into a valuable resource. It's about proving that even the smallest creatures can make a big impact.

So, my friends, take up the challenge and dive into the mesmerizing world of vermiculture. Embrace the worms, become their ally, and together, we'll build a greener, more sustainable future. Happy composting!

BUILDING your vermiculture system is not just about composting; it's about embracing the complexity of nature, questioning conventional waste management methods, and appreciating the tireless work of earthworms. With a sense of curiosity and the right tools, you can become a vermicomposting superhero, making a positive impact on the environment while creating nutrient-rich compost for your garden. So, roll up your sleeves, grab a worm bin, and let the composting adventure begin!

Creating the Perfect Home for Your Worms: Vermiculture Bedding and Bed Preparation

UNDERSTANDING the art of vermiculture bedding and bed preparation will not only provide a thriving environment for your wriggly friends but also supercharge your vermicomposting efforts, producing nutrient-rich humus for your plants. Get ready to unlock the secrets of successful vermicomposting!

EXPLORING **Suitable Bedding Materials for Vermiculture:** Choosing the right bedding material is crucial for your worm bin's success. Optimal bedding should retain moisture, provide proper aeration, and offer a comfortable dwelling for the worms. The key is to strike a balance between carbon-rich and nitrogen-rich materials. Common bedding options include shredded news-paper, cardboard, coconut coir, and aged compost. Each has its benefits and considerations, so let's explore them in detail.

PREPARING **the Bedding for Your Worms:** Now that you've selected your bedding materials, it's time to prepare the worm bin. Proper preparation ensures that your worms have the best start possible. First, moisten the bedding material until it reaches the consistency of a wrung-out sponge. Avoid sogginess, as this can drown the worms. Fluff up the bedding to create air pockets for improved aeration, which is vital for your worms' respiration. Remember, a well-prepared bedding sets the foundation for your worms' thriving home.

MAINTAINING **Optimal Moisture and Aeration Levels:** A critical aspect of vermicomposting is maintaining the right mois-ture and aeration levels. Too much moisture can lead to a lack of oxygen, potentially harming the worms, while insufficient mois-ture can hinder decomposition. To maintain the balance, regu-larly check the bedding's moisture level and adjust as needed. Sprinkle water when it feels dry, and add more dry bedding if it becomes too wet. Fluff the bedding periodically to promote air circulation and prevent compaction. Your worms will happily feast on a well-ventilated, perfectly moist environment.

Troubleshooting and Tips for Success

. . .

EVEN WITH THE BEST PREPARATIONS, challenges may arise during vermiculture. But fear not! Here are some common issues you may encounter and tips to overcome them:

- **Foul Odors:** If you notice unpleasant smells emanating from your worm bin, it's a sign of overfeeding or excessive moisture. Adjust your feeding habits and add more dry bedding to counterbalance the moisture.
- **Fruit Flies or Gnats:** These pesky insects can be a result of overripe fruits or vegetables in the bin. Be mindful of your worm bin's diet and avoid putting in large quantities of food at once.
- **Worm Migration:** Sometimes, worms may try to escape the bin. Ensure the bin is well-covered and check if any environmental factors are causing discomfort.
- **Harvesting the Compost:** When it's time to harvest the compost, move the contents of the bin to one side and add fresh bedding and food to the other. The worms will naturally migrate, making it easier to collect the nutrient-rich compost.

BY SELECTING SUITABLE MATERIALS, preparing the bedding properly, and maintaining ideal moisture and aeration levels, you've created the perfect home for your worms to thrive. Embrace the exciting process of vermicomposting, and witness nature's magic as your worms transform kitchen scraps into valuable compost for your garden.

Selecting and Introducing Earthworms: Understanding the characteristics of suitable earthworm species

. . .

COME across the vital aspects of selecting and introducing earthworms into your vermicomposting system. Understanding the characteristics of suitable earthworm species is the first step towards creating a thriving composting ecosystem that will enrich your garden and reduce waste.

CHOOSING the right earthworm species is essential for the success of your vermicomposting venture. Let's explore some key characteristics to consider when making your selection. By the end of this step, you'll have a clear understanding of what to look for in your composting companions and how it will benefit your efforts.

ECO-FRIENDLY WASTE MANAGERS: Earthworms are nature's little waste managers, but not all species are equally effective. Red Wigglers (Eisenia fetida) and European Nightcrawlers (Eisenia hortensis) are among the top choices for vermicomposting due to their voracious appetites and rapid reproduction rates. These eco-friendly champions will efficiently consume organic waste, leaving behind nutrient-rich castings.

CLIMATE ADAPTABILITY: Consider the climate in your region and choose earthworm species that can thrive in the conditions you provide. Red Wigglers prefer moderate temperatures, making them ideal for indoor vermicomposting setups. On the other hand, European Nightcrawlers can withstand cooler temperatures, making them a great choice for outdoor composting in milder climates.

SOURCING High-quality Worms for your Vermicomposting System: Now that you're familiar with the characteristics of suitable earthworm species, let's move on to the crucial step of sourcing high-quality worms for your vermicomposting system. Acquiring healthy and vibrant worms is essential for jumpstarting your compost successfully. In this step, we'll explore where and how to find these wonderful little recyclers and set you on the path to composting excellence.

LOCAL WORM SUPPLIERS: Start your search by looking for local worm suppliers or vermicomposting enthusiasts in your area. Purchasing worms from nearby sources ensures that they are acclimated to the local environment, increasing their chances of thriving in your composting system.

ONLINE WORM RETAILERS: If local options are limited, reputable online worm retailers are a fantastic alternative. When choosing an online seller, read reviews and check for customer satisfaction to ensure you're getting healthy and happy worms.

WORM QUALITY: When receiving your worms, inspect their condition carefully. They should be lively, moist, and free from foul odors. If you notice any issues, promptly contact the seller for replacements. Now comes the exciting part: introducing and acclimating them to their new environment. This step is vital to ensure your worms settle in comfortably and start their waste-munching promptly.

PREPARING THE HABITAT: Before introducing your worms, ensure that their new home is ready. Line the vermicomposting bin with moistened shredded newspaper or coconut coir to create a cozy bedding for them. Avoid using materials like glossy paper or cardboard, as they may be harmful to your composting friends.

SLOW AND STEADY INTRODUCTION: Gently place the worms on top of the bedding and let them burrow in naturally. Avoid dumping them all in one spot, as this may cause stress and competition among the worms. Let them settle in at their own pace.

FEEDING PRACTICES: Initially, feed your worms small amounts of kitchen scraps, such as fruit and vegetable peels. As they get accustomed to their new home, gradually increase the amount of food waste. Remember, moderation is key – overfeeding can lead to issues like foul odors and fruit fly infestations.

IN CONCLUSION, understanding the characteristics of suitable earthworm species, sourcing high-quality worms, and introducing them to their new environment are critical steps in successful vermicomposting. By following these guidelines, you'll be well on your way to creating nutrient-rich compost for your garden while minimizing waste.

Feeding Your Earthworms: Identifying the Best Food Sources for Your Worms

TAKE a tour on the crucial aspect of feeding your earthworms to achieve efficient composting. Understanding the right food sources for your worms is key to maintaining a thriving worm bin and producing nutrient-rich vermicompost for your garden. So, let's dive in and discover how to keep those earthworms well-fed and happy!

FEEDING your worms might seem straightforward, but there are some essential considerations to keep in mind. By the end of this guide, you'll be well-equipped with a feeding routine that fosters healthy worm activity and prevents common pitfalls.

. . .

WHY PROPER FEEDING MATTERS: Before we dig into the nitty-gritty, let's understand why proper feeding is crucial for your composting venture. Earthworms are exceptional decomposers; they consume organic matter and transform it into valuable compost filled with nutrients that plants love. Feeding them the right mix of materials not only aids their well-being but also enhances the composting process.

Finding the Right Balance

AS YOU SET out to feed your earthworms, remember that moderation is key. A balanced diet contributes to a healthy worm population and efficient composting. You can offer a wide variety of food scraps, but it's essential to maintain the right balance between "greens" and "browns."

GREENS INCLUDE nitrogen-rich materials like fruit and vegetable scraps, coffee grounds, and tea bags. These provide essential nutrients to your worms, promoting rapid decomposition.

BROWNS ENCOMPASS carbon-rich items such as shredded newspaper, cardboard, and dried leaves. Browns create a suitable bedding environment and prevent the worm bin from becoming too acidic.

Creating a Feeding Routine

ESTABLISHING a feeding routine is essential for managing your worm bin effectively. Consistency is key here. Consider feeding your earthworms small amounts of food regularly rather than large quantities infrequently.

. . .

STEP 1: **Prepare Food Scraps**

Chop or shred food scraps into smaller pieces to accelerate decomposition and make them easier for the worms to consume. Smaller scraps provide a larger surface area for the worms to work their magic.

STEP 2: **Bury the Food Scraps**

Create a small hole in the worm bedding and bury the food scraps beneath the surface. This helps control odor and prevents fruit flies or other pests from being attracted to the bin.

STEP 3: **Monitor Consumption**

Observe how quickly your worms consume the food scraps. If there are still leftovers from the previous feeding, reduce the amount next time. Adjusting the feeding amount based on your worm's consumption rate ensures they get the right amount of food without causing any waste.

Avoiding Common Feeding Mistakes

TO MAINTAIN A THRIVING WORM BIN, it's essential to avoid common feeding mistakes. Here are some pitfalls to steer clear of:

- **Overfeeding:** This can lead to food scraps rotting in the worm bin, causing foul odors and attracting pests. Stick to the "less is more" approach and add more food only when the previous scraps are mostly consumed.
- **Unsuitable Foods:** Certain foods are unsuitable for worm consumption, such as meat, dairy, oily foods,

and pet waste. These can attract pests and disrupt the delicate balance of the worm bin.

- **Acidic Foods:** Highly acidic foods like citrus peels and onions should be added in moderation. Too much acidity can harm the worms and slow down the composting process.

FEEDING your earthworms may appear simple, but it's an art that requires attention and care. By identifying appropriate food sources, establishing a feeding routine, and avoiding common mistakes, you'll be well on your way to successful vermicomposting. Remember, happy worms mean nutrient-rich compost for your garden and a positive impact on the environment.

earthworm care and
maintenance

. . .

YOU'VE EMBRACED the art of worm composting, and now you're the proud caregiver of a bustling worm bin full of squirming soil superheroes. But wait, before you start envisioning your garden blooming with bountiful produce, it's time to dive into the world of earthworm care and maintenance. Trust me, these little wrigglers are more than just a "set it and forget it" addition to your sustainability arsenal.

WHY SHOULD you care about caring for your composting worms? Well, my friend, it's simple - happy worms mean a thriving composting system, and a thriving composting system means nutrient-rich, black gold for your plants. It's a win-win situation, and you get to be the hero who ensures your wormy pals have all they need to work their composting magic.

WORM B&B: Just like us humans, worms need a comfortable home. Make sure their humble abode, the worm bin, provides all the creature comforts they crave. Adequate ventilation, moisture, and bedding are essential to keep these tiny ecological warriors content.

. . .

BEDDING MATTERS: Think of worm bedding as a five-star hotel's fluffy pillows and crisp linens. Shredded newspaper, cardboard, or coconut coir are perfect worm bedding materials. Keep it moist but not soggy - worms aren't fans of waterlogged suites!

MIND THE MENU: You are what you eat, and the same goes for worms. Remember, they're vegetarians! Feed them a well-balanced diet of kitchen scraps like fruit and veggie peels, coffee grounds, and tea bags. Your worms will happily dine on this delicious organic buffet.

MODERATION IS KEY: As much as worms love a good feast, too much of a good thing can be a problem. Overfeeding can lead to stinky bins and potential worm exodus. Gauge your worm's appetite and adjust their meals accordingly.

TEMPERATURE TANGO: Worms are nature's Goldilocks; they like it not too hot, not too cold, but just right. Aim for a temperature range of 55-77°F (13-25°C) to keep your wormy friends in the comfort zone.

HIDE AND SEEK: Worms are quite the shy bunch, preferring darkness and solitude. Keep your worm bin in a shaded, quiet spot away from direct sunlight and foot traffic. Let them work their composting magic in peace.

SQUEEZE TEST: Don't worry; you won't be squeezing the worms themselves! However, a handy trick to monitor moisture levels is the "squeeze test." Grab a handful of bedding and give it a gentle squeeze. If a few drops of water emerge, you're good to go!

Now, you might be wondering, "Why all the fuss? Aren't worms supposed to be resilient creatures?" Yes, worms are hardy, but even the mightiest of superheroes need some love and care. Treating your composting worms with respect ensures they perform at their best, transforming your kitchen scraps into the best darn compost your garden has ever seen!

THINK of worm care as a dance between you and your wiggly companions. Pay attention to their needs, and they'll reward you with buckets of nutrient-rich castings and a thriving composting ecosystem. You'll witness the magic of a symbiotic relationship between human and worm - a feedback loop of mutual support and growth.

So, go forth and embrace your role as the guardian of your composting worms. Show them that you care, and they'll reciprocate in ways that will leave your garden greener and your heart fuller.

Now, take a moment to reflect on this newfound connection with the tiny but mighty earthworms. As you nurture them, you're nurturing the soil, the plants, and the environment at large. Embrace this small act of stewardship, for it's through these seemingly ordinary gestures that we can create an extraordinary impact on the world around us.

IN THE SYMPHONY OF SUSTAINABILITY, you've found your melody with worm composting - a tune that resonates with the rhythms of nature. As you continue in nurturing your composting companions, remember that it's the simplest actions that often yield the most profound results.

So, my fellow worm whisperer, let's embark on this adventure with our wiggly garden warriors by our side. Together, we'll compost, cultivate, and champion a greener, more harmonious planet.

. . .

Composting Guide: Monitoring and Maintaining Moisture Levels

WHETHER YOU'RE a seasoned vermiculture enthusiast or just starting, understanding and implementing proper moisture conditions is key to a thriving worm composting system. Think about a composting process that's efficient, odor-free, and produces rich, nutrient-dense vermicompost for your plants and garden. That's exactly what we'll achieve together through this comprehensive guide.

Assessing the Moisture Requirements of Your Worm Composting System

UNDERSTAND the importance of moisture in the composting process. Learn how to gauge moisture levels using simple techniques. Recognize the signs of both dry and overly moist conditions.

Strategies for Maintaining Optimal Moisture Conditions

DISCOVER effective methods to add moisture when it's too dry. Explore various ways to reduce excess moisture in your composting system. Learn about moisture-holding materials to use in your worm bin.

Troubleshooting Common Moisture-Related Issues

. . .

ADDRESS POTENTIAL PROBLEMS, such as foul odors and fruit fly infestations. Find solutions to prevent your compost from becoming too soggy or too dry. Implement preventative measures to avoid recurring issues.

YOU OPEN YOUR WORM BIN, and instead of the earthy smell of healthy compost, you're hit with a rancid stench. This could be a sign of excess moisture, which not only attracts pests but also indicates potential harm to your worms. To avoid this, ensure proper drainage in your worm bin and add bedding materials like shredded newspaper or coconut coir to absorb excess moisture.

EVER WONDERED why your worms seem sluggish and uninterested in composting? Have you experienced the frustration of your compost drying out too quickly? Fear not! We'll address these common concerns and help you troubleshoot any moisture-related issues along the way.

BY NOW, you've gained valuable insights into monitoring and maintaining moisture levels in your worm composting system. Armed with this knowledge, you can confidently embark on a composting adventure that's efficient, odor-free, and eco-friendly. So, go forth, compost with gusto, and let your garden thrive with nutrient-rich vermicompost!

Monitoring and Maintaining Moisture Levels: Assessing the Moisture Requirements of Your Worm Composting System

THE NATURE'S little helpers work their magic to turn kitchen scraps into nutrient-rich compost for your plants. In this section, we'll dive into the crucial aspect of monitoring and maintaining moisture levels in your worm composting system. By the end, you'll be equipped with the knowledge to ensure your worms thrive and produce that "black gold" compost.

MOISTURE IS the lifeblood of a successful worm composting system. It plays a pivotal role in aiding decomposition, promoting a healthy worm population, and preventing odor issues. Striking the right balance of moisture is the key to unlocking the full potential of your composting efforts.

Assessing Moisture Requirements

YOUR WORM BIN AS A COZY, damp environment—just like a wrung-out sponge. When you press the bedding material, a few drops of water should be released, but it shouldn't be dripping wet. To assess the moisture level accurately, follow these simple steps:

- **The Squeeze Test:** Take a handful of bedding material and gently squeeze it. It should feel like a damp sponge, with moisture evenly distributed.
- **Visual Cues:** Observe the bedding's appearance. If you see pools of water or excess liquid draining, it's a sign of excessive moisture. Conversely, if the bedding looks dry and crumbly, it's time to add some water.
- **Check the Odor:** A well-balanced compost bin should have an earthy, pleasant smell. Foul odors indicate that your bin might be too wet or lacking airflow.

REMEMBER, understanding your compost's moisture needs is fundamental to its success!

Strategies for Maintaining Optimal Moisture Conditions

NOW THAT YOU'VE assessed your compost's moisture levels, let's explore some effective strategies to maintain the perfect balance:

- **Add Water Gradually:** When adding water to your bin, do it gradually and evenly. Spread the water across the surface to ensure it's well-distributed throughout the bedding.
- **Use a Spray Bottle:** A spray bottle comes in handy for misting the bedding, preventing over-saturation. It allows you to control the moisture level more precisely.
- **Cover Your Bin:** Use a breathable lid or cover to retain moisture and maintain a stable environment for your worms.
- **Collect Rainwater:** Consider collecting rainwater for your composting needs. Rainwater is free from chlorine and other chemicals found in tap water, making it ideal for your worm friends.
- **Keep an Eye on the Weather:** Be mindful of weather conditions, especially during rainy seasons. You might need to adjust your watering frequency accordingly.

Troubleshooting Common Moisture-Related Issues

Despite your best efforts, sometimes moisture issues can still arise. Here are some common problems and how to tackle them:

- **Excessive Moisture:** If your bin becomes too wet, add dry bedding material like shredded newspaper or cardboard. These will help absorb excess water and restore the balance.
- **Foul Odors:** Foul smells are often a sign of poor aeration and excess moisture. Mix the bedding thoroughly to improve airflow and consider adding more dry, carbon-rich materials like leaves or straw.
- **Dry Bin:** If your bin is too dry, moisten the bedding by spraying it with water. Alternatively, you can place a damp cloth or paper towel on top of the bedding to introduce some moisture.

By understanding the importance of proper moisture, implementing effective strategies, and troubleshooting common issues, you're well on your way to becoming a composting pro. Remember, happy worms lead to exceptional compost, benefiting both your garden and the environment.

Pest Management in Vermiculture: Identifying and Controlling Pests to Ensure Healthy Vermiculture

Pests can pose significant threats to your hardworking worms, affecting the overall health and efficiency of your composting process. But fear not! By understanding common pests and adopting preventive measures, you can maintain a thriving worm ecosystem, ensuring your vermicomposting smooth and successful.

Identifying Common Pests and Potential Threats to Your Worms

LET'S begin by familiarizing ourselves with the common culprits that might sneak into your worm bin. These pests can include fruit flies, mites, ants, and even larger creatures like rodents. Understanding the potential threats they pose is crucial in safeguarding your worms.

YOU'VE GOT a thriving vermicomposting setup, and suddenly, you notice tiny fruit flies buzzing around your bin. They might seem harmless at first, but they can multiply rapidly, competing with your worms for food and laying eggs in the organic matter. This can disrupt the composting process and cause stress to your worm buddies.

Preventive Measures for Keeping Pests Away from Your Vermicomposting System

NOW THAT WE know the pesky intruders, it's time to fortify your vermicomposting fortress. Prevention is key! The best defense is creating an inhospitable environment for pests while keeping your worms comfortable and content.

ONE PRACTICAL APPROACH is to cover your worm bin with a tight-fitting lid to prevent flies and other insects from gaining entry. Additionally, consider elevating the bin on a stand, as this will make it less accessible to crawling pests like ants. Remember to store your food scraps in a sealed container before adding them to the bin, as this will discourage fruit flies from laying eggs in the fresh food.

Safe and Effective Methods to Control Pests Without Harming the Worms

DESPITE YOUR BEST EFFORTS, some pests may still find their way into your vermicomposting haven. But worry not! We've got you covered with safe and eco-friendly pest control methods that won't harm your beloved worms.

FOR INSTANCE, introducing natural predators like nematodes can help control pests like mites and other harmful insects. These beneficial microorganisms will seek out and devour the unwanted guests, keeping your worm bin pest-free. Another effective approach is diatomaceous earth, a fine powder derived from fossilized algae. It acts as a natural insecticide by dehydrating pests upon contact, while being harmless to your worms.

WHILE MANAGING pests in vermiculture is relatively straightforward, it's essential to keep an eye on the delicate balance within your worm ecosystem. Overusing chemical pesticides can be harmful to your worms and may disrupt the natural breakdown of organic matter.

REMEMBER, a diverse diet is crucial for your worms' well-being. Avoid overfeeding them, as excess food can attract pests and generate foul odors. If you notice a sudden population explosion of a particular pest, it might be a sign that your compost pile needs adjustment.

YOU NOW HAVE the knowledge and tools to conquer the challenges of pest management in vermiculture. By identifying common pests, taking preventive measures, and employing safe control methods, you'll ensure your worms can work their magic without disturbance.

. . .

KEEP in mind that vermiculture is balance and harmony. Embrace your role as a vermicomposting caretaker, and your worms will reward you with nutrient-rich compost for your garden and a sustainable way to reduce waste.

composting materials
and food sources

. . .

YOU'VE JUST FINISHED DEVOURING a delicious watermelon on a scorching summer day. Instead of discarding the rinds, you toss them into your compost bin. A few weeks later, those rinds decompose, and the once discarded organic matter becomes a powerful elixir for your garden, teeming with beneficial microorganisms and nutrients. It's a win-win situation—less waste in landfills, healthier soil, and thriving greenery.

COMPOSTING IS like performing a magic trick that's also an act of rebellion against wasteful habits. It's a slap in the face of conventional wisdom that encourages tossing everything into the trash without a second thought. Why should we let our kitchen scraps and yard waste rot in a landfill, producing harmful greenhouse gases, when they can work their transformative wonders in our very own backyards?

Now, you might be thinking, "Composting? That's for the granola-eating, tree-hugging, hippie types." But let me tell you, composting is a superhero solution that appeals to both the environmentally conscious and the financially savvy. It doesn't matter if you're a broke college student or a budding entrepreneur; composting is the equalizer in the world of sustainable living.

FOR THOSE WITH A BACKYARD, this traditional method involves a compost bin or heap. Toss in yard waste, kitchen scraps, and a dash of patience, and let nature do the rest. Don't have a backyard? No problem! Try worm composting (vermicomposting) with a worm bin. Let those wiggly critters munch on your food scraps and turn them into valuable worm castings.

ALMOST ANYTHING that was once alive can join the compost party! Fruit and vegetable scraps, coffee grounds, tea bags, eggshells, yard trimmings, and shredded paper. Additionally, meat, dairy, oily foods, pet waste, and diseased plants. They're the party poopers of composting, attracting pests and creating funky smells.

LIKE A SKILLED CHEF, balance is key. A successful compost pile needs a mix of green (nitrogen-rich) and brown (carbon-rich) materials. Think of it as a dance between the fresh green waste and the dried brown leaves, with the microorganisms as the DJ!

BEFORE YOU DISMISS COMPOSTING as just another trendy eco-hack, let's talk about the impact. According to the Environmental Protection Agency, almost 30% of household waste is compostable. The positive change we can create if each one of us embraced composting as a daily ritual!

So, go forth, young composter, and unleash the alchemy of sustainability in your life. Turn your kitchen scraps into a symphony of life and vitality in your garden. Challenge the status quo, and let's compost our way to a greener, healthier future, one banana peel at a time!

Organic Waste for Vermicomposting: Turning Trash into Black Gold

A SUSTAINABLE WAY TO manage kitchen scraps, yard waste, and other biodegradable materials while simultaneously enriching your soil and reducing landfill waste. In this guide, we will dive into the vast array of organic materials suitable for vermicomposting, understand the crucial carbon-to-nitrogen ratio, and categorize compostable items into greens, browns, and other essentials.

Exploring Organic Materials for Vermicomposting

WE WILL UNVEIL the treasure trove of organic materials that can become valuable compost. Kitchen scraps like fruit and vegetable peels, coffee grounds, and eggshells are prime candidates. Garden waste, such as grass clippings and plant trimmings, also make excellent additions to your vermicomposting bin. Even paper products like shredded newspaper and cardboard can play a role. The key is to avoid meat, dairy, and oily foods, which can attract pests and slow down the composting process.

Understanding the Carbon-to-Nitrogen Ratio

AH, the magical balance of the carbon-to-nitrogen ratio – the secret sauce behind successful vermicomposting. Greens are nitrogen-rich materials that provide protein for the worms, while browns are carbon-rich materials that act as a source of energy. Finding the right balance between greens and browns is essential for efficient composting. Aim for a ratio of 2:1, with slightly more browns to prevent a smelly and slimy mess. Striking this harmony allows the worms to thrive and work their composting magic. For an instance, think of greens as the protein-packed greens in a healthy salad and browns as the energy-rich grains that keep you going!

Categorizing Compostable Items

IN THIS STEP, we'll categorize the materials you can compost into greens, browns, and other compostable items. Greens include nitrogen-rich items like fruit scraps, vegetable peels, and coffee grounds, while browns encompass carbon-rich materials like dried leaves, straw, and cardboard. Additionally, other compostable items, such as eggshells, hair, and even fireplace ashes, can enhance your compost mix. Understanding these categories will help you create a diverse and well-balanced compost blend. Additionally, greens and browns are like the yin and yang of vermicomposting, while other compostable items add unique flavors to the mix!

NOW THAT YOU'VE got the basics down, let's dive deeper into practical tips for a successful vermicomposting. Keep your compost moist, but not waterlogged, as worms require a comfortable environment to thrive. Avoid adding too much citrus or onions to the mix, as worms are not fans of these strong odors. Occasionally, give your worms a treat by adding small amounts of crushed eggshells for grit, promoting their digestion.

THROUGH EXPLORING ORGANIC MATERIALS, understanding the carbon-to-nitrogen ratio, and categorizing compostable items, you've taken a giant leap towards sustainable living and reducing your carbon footprint. Embrace this eco-friendly practice, and let your worms work their magic, transforming your trash into nutrient-rich black gold.

Preparing and Processing Compostable Materials: A Comprehensive Guide to Sustainable Composting

DISCOVER the exciting process of preparing and processing compostable materials. By understanding and implementing these steps, you'll not only contribute to a greener planet but also enjoy the benefits of nutrient-rich compost to enhance your garden and plants. Let's embark on composting together!

Preparing and Shredding Larger Compostable Items for Faster Decomposition

TO KICKSTART OUR COMPOSTING ADVENTURE, let's focus on breaking down larger compostable items effectively. By shredding them into smaller pieces, we accelerate the decomposition process. The quicker your compost will be ready with this simple technique! So, grab your shredder and get ready to transform your kitchen scraps and garden waste into black gold.

Utilizing Different Techniques to Accelerate the Breakdown of Organic Waste

COMPOSTING IS NOT JUST a one-size-fits-all approach. We'll explore various composting techniques to suit your preferences and needs. From traditional bin composting to innovative methods like hot composting and bokashi composting, we've got you covered. Understanding these techniques will help you find the best fit for your lifestyle and composting goals.

Properly Layering and Mixing Compostable Materials in the Vermicomposting System

VERMICOMPOSTING, also known as worm composting, is a fantastic way to compost indoors and even with limited space. But how do you ensure your worms are happy and your compost is thriving? It all comes down to proper layering and mixing. We'll guide you through the process of creating a cozy worm habitat and how to maintain the perfect balance of food scraps and bedding.

EVER WONDERED if you can compost those avocado pits or leftover coffee grounds? Well, stay tuned because we've got the answers! Discover the surprising compostable items that you never knew could go into your compost pile.

REMEMBER TO AVOID ADDING MEAT, dairy, and oily foods to your compost. These can attract unwanted pests and slow down the decomposition process. Stick to vegetable scraps, fruit peels, coffee filters, and eggshells for a thriving compost pile.

NOTE that it's a rewarding process that benefits both you and the environment. By preparing and processing compostable materials correctly, you'll witness the transformation of waste into valuable compost, nourishing the soil and promoting healthy plant growth. So, start composting today and join the green movement that's shaping a sustainable future for all!

REMEMBER, composting is not just a chore; it's an exciting adventure that brings us closer to nature and the circle of life. Happy composting, and may your garden bloom with life and vitality!

Nourishing the Earth: Avoiding Harmful Substances in Worm Feed

IF YOU'RE into vermicomposting and looking to take your composting game to the next level, understanding the impact of certain chemicals on the process is crucial. In this section, we'll explore how to recognize materials toxic to worms, discover the implications of harmful substances on the vermicomposting process, and learn best practices to maintain a safe composting environment. By the end, you'll be equipped to ensure your worm friends thrive and produce top-notch compost!

Recognizing Materials Toxic to Worms

WE FIRST NEED to be vigilant about the materials we introduce to our worm bins. Some substances can be harmful, even deadly, to our wriggly companions. Keeping a keen eye out for these materials can save you and your worms from unnecessary trouble. Here are some things to look out for:

- **No-no Foods for Worms:** Some foods should never find their way into your worm bin, like citrus fruits, onions, garlic, and spicy foods. Worms find these acidic or pungent foods intolerable, and it can disrupt the composting process.
- **Toxic Chemicals:** Avoid materials treated with pesticides, herbicides, or other harmful chemicals. These substances can harm the worms directly or disrupt the delicate balance of the composting process.

Understanding the Impact of Harmful Chemicals on Vermicomposting

Now THAT WE know what to avoid let's dive deeper into why these materials are problematic. Understanding the consequences of introducing harmful substances into your worm bin will empower you to make informed decisions. Knowledge is power, after all!

- **Disturbance to Worm Ecosystem:** Worms are incredibly sensitive creatures. Toxic substances can disrupt their living conditions, causing stress, reduced reproduction rates, and even death. We want a happy worm community, don't we?
- **Disruption of Composting Process:** Harmful chemicals can interfere with the natural breakdown of organic matter, negatively impacting the composting process. This means slower decomposition and lower-quality compost.

Best Practices for a Safe Composting Environment

Now THAT WE'RE aware of the potential dangers, let's focus on maintaining a safe and productive composting environment for our worms. By following these best practices, you can ensure your worms thrive and create nutrient-rich compost:

- **Use Worm-Friendly Feed:** Stick to a balanced diet of vegetable scraps, fruit peels, coffee grounds, and crushed eggshells. This will keep your worms happy and the composting process running smoothly.

- **Compost Pre-Processing:** Before adding any new material to your worm bin, ensure it's free from harmful chemicals. This might mean washing, chopping, or simply allowing certain materials to decompose for a while.
- **Monitor Worm Behavior:** Keep a close eye on your worm bin and observe your little composting engineers. If you notice any unusual behavior, it could be a sign of distress or contamination.
- **Maintain Proper Moisture Levels:** Worms need a moist environment to breathe and move comfortably. Regularly check the moisture level in your worm bin and adjust as needed.

You're now well-equipped to safeguard your worms from harmful substances and create a thriving vermicomposting environment. By recognizing what to avoid, understanding the impact of harmful substances, and implementing best practices, you can ensure your worms' well-being and produce high-quality compost.

harvesting and utilizing vermicompost

. . .

Unlocking the Secret Sauce for Lush Greenery
and Sustainable Living

GONE ARE the days of resorting to chemical fertilizers that
harm the environment and deplete the soil of its natural goodness. Vermicompost is the eco-friendly, sustainable, and down-
right cool way to nourish your plants and Mother Earth
simultaneously.

WHY SHOULD YOU CARE?

ARE you tired of struggling to keep your plants alive despite your
best efforts? Do you feel like your green thumb is more of a
brownish hue? Vermicompost is the ultimate secret weapon to
turn your gardening game around and bring life back to your
beloved plants. Say goodbye to wilted leaves and withered stems;
say hello to thriving greenery that will make your neighbors turn
green with envy!

AND HEY, this isn't just about pretty flowers and succulent
veggies; it's a full-fledged lifestyle overhaul! By embracing vermicomposting, you're joining the ranks of the eco-conscious, the
planet's defenders, and the sustainability aficionados. It's like

becoming a gardening superhero – your cape might not be as flashy, but your impact on the environment will be extraordinary.

LET'S TALK ABOUT WORMS, those unassuming yet indispensable creatures that are busy working behind the scenes to save the planet. They munch on your kitchen scraps, newspaper shreds, and cardboard leftovers, and what do they produce? Pure magic – vermicompost! It's a glorious cycle of waste turning into wonder.

DON'T UNDERESTIMATE the power of these slimy superheroes. Charles Darwin himself once said, "It may be doubted whether there are many other animals which have played so important a part in the history of the world as these lowly organized creatures." Who knew that worms had a cult following among the intellectual elite?

NOW THAT YOU'RE excited about starting your vermicomposting, it's time to get your hands dirty – literally! Don't fret; this isn't rocket science. With just a few easy steps, you'll be well on your way to producing the black gold that your plants crave.

- **Worm Bin Selection:** Choose a suitable worm bin; it could be a commercially available one or a DIY project. Get creative, and remember that worms are low-maintenance creatures, so they won't mind if you repurpose an old container.
- **Bedding is Key:** Your worms need a cozy bed to thrive. Use shredded newspaper, cardboard, or coconut coir as bedding – it's like a five-star worm hotel!
- **Worms Move In:** Invite your wormy friends into their new home. Red wrigglers are the rock stars of the vermicomposting world, so make sure to invite them to the party.

- **Feeding Frenzy:** Time to feed your worms with kitchen scraps like fruit and veggie peels, coffee grounds, and tea bags. No meat or dairy, though; let's keep the menu healthy and vegan.
- **Chillax and Harvest:** Now, sit back and let the worms do their thing. In a few months, you'll have a bin full of nutrient-rich vermicompost ready to nourish your plants.

REMEMBER, vermicomposting isn't just a one-and-done deal; it's a feedback loop of goodness. The more compost you make, the healthier your plants become, and the more organic waste you divert from landfills. It's a win-win for you and the planet!

BUT WAIT, There's More!

IF YOU THOUGHT VERMICOMPOSTING WAS LIMITED to just enriching your garden, think again! This magical potion has more tricks up its sleeve. You can brew worm tea – not the kind you'd serve at a Mad Hatter's tea party, mind you. Worm tea is the liquid gold that your plants will chug happily. Dilute it with water, and watch your greens grow with gusto!

SO THERE YOU HAVE IT – the captivating world of vermicomposting laid bare. The power of worms and organic waste coming together to create something beautiful, sustainable, and oh-so-enriching. Embrace this green revolution and join the ranks of gardening superheroes. Let's make the world a greener place, one worm at a time!

Gardeners' Guide: How to Recognize When Worm Castings are Ready for Your Plants

. . .

WORMS WORK their magic to transform organic waste into nutrient-rich worm castings. Unravel the art of recognizing when those precious castings are fully ready for use. Understanding the maturity and readiness of vermicompost is crucial for gardeners and plant enthusiasts seeking to enrich their soil and foster thriving plant life. Get ready to discover the physical characteristics of fully composted worm castings and learn how to identify signs of unfinished composting or potential issues with the process. By the end, you'll be a master at discerning those luscious, black gold pellets, so let's dive in!

Indicators to Determine Maturity and Readiness

- **Visual Inspection:** The first step in recognizing mature worm castings is a visual inspection. Fully composted worm castings should have a dark, rich color, resembling crumbly soil. They should be free from any recognizable food scraps or bedding materials.
- **Earthy Aroma:** Ready-to-use worm castings emit an earthy, pleasant smell similar to fresh soil. If you detect any foul odors, it's a sign that the composting process might not be complete or that something has gone awry.
- **Texture and Consistency:** Mature worm castings should have a fine texture, like coffee grounds. They should be crumbly to the touch and easy to work with, indicating that they are well-processed and teeming with beneficial microorganisms.

Understanding Physical Characteristics

. . .

- **Nutrient Concentration:** One of the defining traits of fully composted worm castings is their exceptional nutrient content. They are packed with essential nutrients such as nitrogen, phosphorus, potassium, and trace minerals that nourish plants and promote robust growth.
- **Microbial Activity:** Healthy worm castings are teaming with beneficial bacteria and microorganisms. These tiny helpers aid in breaking down organic matter further, releasing nutrients in a form that plants can readily absorb.

Identifying Signs of Unfinished Composting or Potential Issues

- **Recognizing Unprocessed Materials:** If you spot recognizable food scraps, bedding materials, or even live worms in the castings, they are not yet mature. Worm castings should be free from any remnants of the initial composting ingredients.
- **Unpleasant Odors:** Foul or putrid odors coming from your worm castings are a clear sign of improper composting. It could be due to overfeeding, excess moisture, or insufficient aeration. Adjust your composting practices to rectify these issues.
- **Pests and Pathogens:** While vermicompost should be rich in beneficial microorganisms, it should not harbor pests or harmful pathogens. If you notice an infestation or signs of disease, it's essential to address the problem promptly.

YOU'VE NOW BECOME a worm casting connoisseur, able to recognize the signs of mature and nutrient-rich vermicompost. By understanding the physical characteristics and identifying potential issues, you're equipped to produce the best possible worm castings for your garden. Remember to trust your senses during composting, and soon you'll reap the rewards of your composting prowess.

The Art of Harvesting Vermicompost: Maximizing Worm Magic for Rich, Nutrient-Dense Soil

UNCOVER the secrets of harvesting this black gold created by nature's humble workers - worms. Transforming kitchen scraps and organic waste into a nutrient-rich, garden-enhancing elixir. With the right techniques, you'll unlock the full potential of your vermicompost, nourishing your plants and contributing to a sustainable, eco-friendly lifestyle.

Selecting the Appropriate Method to Separate Worms from Castings

FIRST THINGS FIRST, we must delicately separate the tireless earthworms from their prized vermicompost. Two primary techniques can be employed: the light sorting method and the migration method.

- **Light sorting method:** In this gentle approach, spread your vermicompost on a large flat surface and expose it to light. Worms are photophobic and will instinctively move away from the light, making it easier for you to collect the worm-free vermicompost.

- **Migration method:** To utilize this method, set up a separate bin with fresh bedding and food. Place it atop your existing vermicompost and allow the worms to migrate upward to the new bin. Once the worms have migrated, you can simply scoop out the vermicompost from the original bin.

Manual and Mechanical Techniques for Maximum Yield

HARVESTING VERMICOMPOST CAN BE a delightful combination of manual and mechanical methods. Here's how to proceed:

- **Hand sorting:** Embrace a hands-on approach and gently pick out any remaining worms or large pieces of organic matter from your vermicompost. Be patient and treat these little workers with care!
- **Sifting:** Employ a mesh screen to sift the vermicompost, ensuring a consistent, fine texture for your final product. The screened vermicompost will be a joy to use in your garden.

Cleaning and Refining Vermicompost for Optimal Quality and Usability

TO GUARANTEE TOP-NOTCH VERMICOMPOST, follow these essential steps:

- **Drying:** Spread the freshly harvested vermicompost thinly in the sun to remove excess moisture. This process also helps in eliminating unwanted pests and weed seeds.
- **Aging:** Allow the vermicompost to rest for a few weeks, promoting further decomposition and enhancing its nutrient content.
- **Sieving:** For the ultimate refinement, sieve the aged vermicompost to ensure a uniform texture, free from any clumps or debris.

Practical Advice and Potential Problems

As you start vermicomposting, keep these tips in mind:

- **Avoid overfeeding:** An overwhelmed worm population may not process all the waste efficiently, leading to unpleasant odors and a less effective end product.
- **Maintain proper moisture levels:** Worms prefer a moist environment, but excessive moisture can lead to anaerobic conditions, causing harm to the worms.

Gazing at your flourishing garden, filled with vibrant blooms and thriving vegetables, all thanks to the magic of vermicompost. Are you ready to unlock the potential of these tiny composting heroes and nurture your plants to their full splendor?

By following these techniques, you'll be able to separate worms from their precious castings, refine the vermicompost to perfection, and elevate your gardening game. Embrace the wonders of nature, and let the wisdom of worms enrich your green endeavors.

Exploring the Magic of Vermicompost: Transform Your Garden and Harvest with Nature's Black Gold

UNRAVEL the fascinating realm of vermicompost, a nutrient-rich fertilizer produced by earthworms. Are you ready to discover how these humble creatures can work wonders for your plants, crops, and soil? Get ready to witness the magic of vermicompost as we explore its applications and benefits!

Understanding Vermicompost: Nature's Black Gold

VERMICOMPOST, also known as worm castings, is a goldmine of nutrients and beneficial microorganisms. But what exactly makes it so precious? Let's unravel its mysteries and grasp why it's a game-changer in gardening and agriculture.

Garden and Agriculture Applications

PREPARE to witness the wonders of vermicompost in action! From vibrant backyard gardens to vast farmlands, we'll explore the diverse applications of vermicompost. Discover how it helps improve plant growth, disease resistance, and overall crop yield, revolutionizing the way we nurture the green world around us.

The Nutritional and Soil-Enhancing Benefits

. . .

LET's dive deeper into the nutritional feast vermicompost offers to your plants. Unearth the essential nutrients that promote healthy root systems, lush foliage, and bountiful harvests. Moreover, we'll explore how vermicompost enhances soil structure, aeration, and water retention, ensuring a thriving ecosystem beneath the surface.

Vermicompost Techniques for Success

IT's time to get your hands dirty! Learn effective techniques to incorporate vermicompost into various growing systems. Whether you're a container gardener, raised bed enthusiast, or traditional farmer, we've got you covered. Discover the dos and don'ts to make the most of this black gold while maintaining a harmonious ecological balance.

THERE MIGHT BE obstacles along the way. Fear not! We'll equip you with practical advice to tackle common challenges when using vermicompost. From potential odor issues to adjusting the composting process, we've got your back on this vermicomposting adventure.

YOU'VE UNLOCKED the secret to a thriving garden and bountiful harvests with vermicompost. By understanding its nutritional benefits and versatile applications, you're well on your way to transforming your gardening and farming practices. Embrace the magic of vermicompost, and let the earthworms work their wonders in harmony with nature. With their help, you'll witness a flourishing, sustainable ecosystem that yields rewards beyond your wildest dreams.

. . .

REMEMBER, this guide is just the beginning of your vermicomposting process. Continuously enrich your knowledge, experiment with different techniques, and share your successes with fellow gardeners and farmers. Together, we'll cultivate a greener, healthier world—one handful of vermicompost at a time.

troubleshooting common issues in vermicomposting

. . .

YOU HAVE AN ARMY OF TINY, wriggly warriors diligently working to turn your kitchen scraps into nutrient-rich black gold. Vermicomposting, the art of harnessing the power of earthworms to break down organic waste, is nothing short of magical. But let's face it, even the most efficient worm soldiers can face their fair share of battles. Fear not, fellow composters! In this chapter, we shall dive deep into the world of vermiculture, exposing its quirks and offering you the knowledge and tools to conquer common challenges. Prepare to become a formidable worm warrior yourself!

The Steamy Love Triangle: Too Hot, Too Cold, Just Right!

- Worms have preferences too! Keep your compost bin's temperature between 55-77°F (13-25°C).
- When things heat up, worms might try to escape like contestants from a reality show. Provide shade and avoid placing the bin in direct sunlight.

- On the flip side, if it's freezing outside, protect your worm buddies by moving the bin indoors or insulating it with cozy blankets.
- Avoid turning your compost bin into a tropical rainforest. Excess moisture can drown the worms and lead to a stinky, anaerobic mess.
- Conversely, bone-dry conditions are no fun either. Maintain the moisture level like the perfect sponge – damp, but not dripping. Your worms appreciate a drink, not a swimming pool!
- Slow down, eager composters! Overfeeding your worms can spell disaster. Remember the golden rule: Worms eat half their weight daily, so match the amount of food they can handle.
- Create a well-balanced menu – mix the green (vegetables, fruits) with the brown (shredded paper, cardboard). Keep the carbon-to-nitrogen ratio happy, and your worms will dine in harmony.
- It's a party, but not everyone is invited. Beware of fruit flies, gnats, and other freeloaders that can crash your worm bin bonanza.
- Keep them out by burying food scraps under the bedding and maintaining a thick, worm-friendly environment.
- Should they still show up, invite some carnivorous plants to the party, they'll take care of the gatecrashers!

EVERY WORM's dream is a buffet of gourmet waste, but it comes with a price – potential imbalance. As some foods are harder to digest, limit the intake of citrus, onions, garlic, and spicy foods. Those might be a bit too spicy for the worms' taste buds.

YOUR WORMS NEED space to wiggle and giggle. Avoid compacting the bedding; they're not fans of crowded dance floors. Provide enough room for the worms to breathe and frolic, and they'll reward you with an astonishing compost party!

Now that you're armed with the wisdom of worm warriors, go forth and conquer the compost pile! But remember, every worm is unique, and sometimes, they might rebel against even the most well-intentioned tactics. Be prepared to adjust your strategy, listen to their tiny whispers, and treat them with the respect they deserve.

In the fascinating world of vermiculture, there's always something new to discover. So, embrace the quirks, roll up your sleeves, and dive into the glorious realm of composting. You are now equipped to troubleshoot like a pro!

As Albert Einstein once said, "Insanity is doing the same thing over and over again and expecting different results." Embrace the change, challenge the status quo, and become a master vermiculturalist! Who knows, your worms might just start singing your praises, and you'll be crowned the worm whisperer in your community.

Embrace the feedback loops in your life, and don't be afraid to adapt and grow alongside your compost pile.

Banish the Stink: Tackling Odor and Foul Smells in Worm Composting

If you're a passionate vermicomposter, you know how fantastic it is to turn kitchen scraps into nutrient-rich compost with the help of our little wriggling friends. However, unpleasant odors can occasionally creep into the process, dampening the experience. But fear not, for in this guide, we'll explore the causes behind these odors and equip you with effective strategies to prevent and eliminate them. With our insights, you'll be able to maintain a fresh and pleasant vermicomposting system that keeps both you and your worms happy!

Identifying the Causes of Unpleasant Odors in Worm Composting

ROTTEN EGG SMELLS? Putrid stench? What's going on in your compost bin? Fear not, we'll explore the culprits behind these odors. Is it excess moisture? Overfeeding the worms? Improper aeration? We've got you covered with simple explanations and easy-to-follow guidelines.

Implementing Strategies to Prevent and Eliminate Odor Issues

NOW THAT WE know the root causes, it's time to take action! From adjusting the moisture levels to finding the right balance of greens and browns, we'll guide you through each step. You'll learn how to create a comfortable home for your worms while keeping unwanted odors at bay.

Troubleshooting Persistent Odor Problems in the Vermicomposting System

UH-OH! Despite your best efforts, the smell lingers. Don't worry; we won't leave you hanging. We'll troubleshoot common issues like anaerobic conditions and compacted bedding, offering practical advice to tackle even the most persistent odors.

Dɪᴅ you know that overfeeding your worms can lead to nasty smells? Remember, moderation is key! Also, keep an eye on moisture levels – worms prefer a damp environment, but too much water can turn their home into a stinky mess. But don't fret! We'll guide you on striking the right balance.

Hᴀᴠᴇ you ever opened your compost bin, only to be met with an unpleasant surprise? We've all been there! But fret not; in the next step, we'll reveal the secret recipe for a sweet-smelling compost bin. Get ready to impress your friends and neighbors with your odor-free composting skills!

Yᴏᴜ ᴄᴀɴ ɴᴏᴡ ᴛʀᴀɴsfᴏʀᴍ your composting system into a fragrant haven. Remember, a little care and attention go a long way in ensuring your composting adventures are fresh and enjoyable. So, go forth and compost with confidence, making the world a greener place—one compost bin at a time!

Managing Moisture Imbalances: Understanding the consequences of excessive moisture or dryness

Gᴇᴛ ᴀ ᴅᴇᴇᴘᴇʀ knowledge on the critical aspect of moisture regulation and how it affects the health and efficiency of your composting process. By the end of this chapter, you'll be equipped with valuable insights and techniques to keep your composting system thriving. Let's dive in!

The Importance of Moisture Balance

. . .

YOUR VERMICOMPOSTING system as a delicate ecosystem that requires the perfect balance to function optimally. Just like Goldilocks, worms prefer their environment not too wet, not too dry, but just right. Excessive moisture can suffocate the worms and lead to unpleasant odors, while dryness inhibits their activity and slows down the decomposition process. Finding the sweet spot is crucial for successful vermicomposting.

Techniques for Adjusting Moisture Levels

To MAINTAIN that ideal moisture balance, here are some practical techniques you can implement:

- **Monitoring Moisture Content:** Regularly check the moisture level of your compost by squeezing a handful of it. It should feel like a wrung-out sponge - damp, but not dripping.
- **Adding Bedding Materials:** Increase moisture levels by incorporating damp bedding materials like shredded newspaper or cardboard. This provides both moisture and carbon-rich materials, making it a win-win for your composting system.
- **Drainage System:** If you notice excess water pooling at the bottom of your compost bin, consider setting up a drainage system. Drill some small holes in the bin's base to allow excess water to escape.

Preventing and Remedying Moisture-Related Problems

EXPERIENCING issues related to moisture in your vermicomposting system? Here's how you can address them:

- **Foul Odors:** If you detect a foul smell emanating from your compost, it's likely due to excessive moisture. To fix this, add dry bedding materials and increase aeration by gently turning the compost with a fork.
- **Mold Growth:** Mold can appear when the compost is too wet and lacks airflow. To combat this, add dry materials and ensure sufficient ventilation by fluffing up the bedding.
- **Dry Compost:** Conversely, if your compost appears dry, sprinkle some water evenly throughout the bin and mix it gently to ensure proper distribution.

Expert Tips for Managing Moisture

HERE ARE some expert tips to help you maintain a healthy moisture balance:

- **Seasonal Adjustments:** Remember that environmental conditions affect moisture levels. In hot and dry weather, you might need to water your compost more frequently, while rainy seasons may require adjustments to prevent excess moisture.
- **Consistency is Key:** Regularly check your compost's moisture level to address imbalances promptly. Consistency in monitoring and adjustments will keep your composting system in top shape.
- **Avoid Overwatering:** Too much water can drown your compost, so be cautious not to overwater, even with good intentions.

. . .

You now have a solid understanding of managing moisture imbalances in your vermicomposting system. By maintaining the right moisture levels, you'll create an environment where worms thrive, decomposition hums along, and compost becomes rich and fertile. Remember, the key is to strike that perfect balance - not too wet, not too dry, but just right.

Pest Control in Vermicomposting: Effective Strategies for a Thriving Ecosystem

Worms turn organic waste into nutrient-rich compost. But just like any thriving ecosystem, vermicomposting can face challenges in the form of pest infestations. Fear not! In this guide, we will explore the impact of common pests on vermicomposting and equip you with natural and organic methods to control and eliminate them. Implementing preventive measures is the key to long-term pest management, ensuring a successful vermicomposting. Let's dive in!

Recognizing Common Pests and Their Impact on Vermicomposting

Before we tackle pest control, it's essential to identify the culprits. Some common pests that may invade your vermicomposting system include fruit flies, ants, mites, and slugs. These critters can disrupt the delicate balance of your worm bin, affecting worm health and compost quality. Understanding their impact empowers you to take timely action.

Natural and Organic Methods to Control and Eliminate Pests in the System

THE BEST WAY to combat pests in vermicomposting is by utilizing nature-friendly techniques. Introduce beneficial predators like nematodes and predatory mites to feast on harmful pests. You can also create physical barriers, such as diatomaceous earth or copper tape, to deter crawling invaders. Additionally, maintaining proper moisture levels and burying food scraps will discourage fruit flies and ants from setting up camp. Remember, a balanced ecosystem is the key to pest control!

Implementing Preventive Measures for Long-Term Pest Management

PREVENTION IS BETTER THAN CURE, and this adage holds true for vermicomposting. Regularly inspect your worm bin to catch early signs of pest activity. Keep the bin covered with a breathable lid to minimize access for flying pests. Make sure the bin is elevated to prevent entry for ground-dwelling insects. Balancing the carbon-to-nitrogen ratio in your compost and avoiding citrus and oily foods will discourage unwanted visitors. By implementing these preventive measures, you can maintain a harmonious environment for your worms.

YOU ARE NOW ARMED with the knowledge to tackle pest infestations in your vermicomposting system effectively. By recognizing common pests, employing natural control methods, and implementing preventive measures, you'll ensure the well-being of your worms and the success of your composting. Remember, pest management is an ongoing process, but with dedication and a watchful eye, you'll create nutrient-rich compost while fostering a thriving ecosystem.

scaling up your
vermiculture operation

. . .

BORED OF THE same old 9-to-5 grind? Tired of the humdrum and itching for a venture that's both fulfilling and eco-friendly? Enter the world of vermiculture - where wriggling worms hold the keys to your success! Yes, you heard it right. In this chapter, we'll dive deep into the earthy secrets of vermicomposting and how you can turn a humble worm farm into a wormpire!

SCALING up your vermiculture operation isn't just about worms and dirt; it's about embracing a sustainable lifestyle and unleashing your inner entrepreneur. Forget about cliché business buzzwords; we're talking about harnessing the power of nature's tiny waste warriors to create organic gold!

YOU MIGHT WONDER, why vermiculture? Well, it's not just about getting your hands dirty and communing with the earthworms (though that's pretty cool). Vermiculture is a green revolution! It's about reducing waste, enhancing soil health, and making moolah while you're at it. And let's face it, it's a surefire way to impress your eco-conscious date at the next farmer's market.

. . .

No, you don't need to go all Dr. Dolittle, but understanding your wriggly employees is crucial. Know their likes (rotting veggies and coffee grounds) and dislikes (spicy salsa, definitely!). Treat your worms right, and they'll reward you with nutrient-rich castings that gardeners will line up for.

VERMICOMPOSTING ISN'T JUST A HOBBY; it's a business opportunity. Embrace your inner wormpreneur and market those worm castings like they're the latest tech gadgets! Your startup might not have flashy offices, but your backyard will become a haven for green enthusiasts.

SCALING UP CAN BE DAUNTING, but don't let it scare you away. Start small and let your worm farm grow organically. Remember, worms aren't the stock market; they won't crash on you overnight. And who knows, your vermiculture empire might soon rival Amazon (okay, maybe that's a stretch).

TO CREATE A WORMPIRE, you need more worms than you can count (but please don't try). Create the perfect breeding conditions, and soon your worm farm will witness a wriggling population explosion! Think of it as a worm rave - minus the glow sticks.

THERE'S something therapeutic about working with worms. Forget yoga, this is the real Zen! Get your hands dirty, breathe in the earthy aroma, and let the stress melt away. Worms are the OG mindfulness coaches.

Now, you might wonder, "Is this all just worm fluff?" Not at all! Experts swear by the power of vermiculture, and influential thinkers have long advocated for eco-friendly solutions like this. As the wise Benjamin Franklin once said, "Worms can do more for a garden than an army."

. . .

But HEY, we get it; embracing vermiculture isn't the norm. People might raise their eyebrows when you tell them about your worm-powered venture. But remember, it's the unconventional ideas that change the world! Who would have thought people would pay big bucks for bottled air or pet rocks?

STILL, like all great endeavors, vermiculture has its challenges. Think of it as a feedback loop; you give the worms love, and they give it back in nutrient-rich castings. Embrace the ups, the downs, and the occasional escapee worms that decide to explore your kitchen.

SCALING up your vermiculture operation is a wild ride, but it's an experience worth taking. It's about challenging the norm, caring for the planet, and making a name for yourself in the green business world. So, let's ditch the clichés and dive into the underground world of vermiculture.

REMEMBER, you don't need a degree in wormology to succeed. Follow the steps, stay true to your vision, and watch your worm empire grow! Your earthy endeavor will not only make a difference but also inspire others to embrace sustainable entrepreneurship.

Now, if you'll excuse us, we've got some worms to talk to and a wormpire to build. As the great worm whisperer once said, "The world is your compost bin, my friend!"

Scaling Up Your Worm Composting Setup: From Small-Scale to Large-Scale Success

IF YOU'VE BEEN SUCCESSFULLY MANAGING a small-scale worm composting system and are now ready to take your eco-friendly endeavors to the next level, you've come to the right place. In this guide, we'll explore the essential considerations, equipment choices, and strategies to smoothly transition from a small-scale setup to a larger-scale system. Scaling up means greater impact and more sustainable practices, and we'll help you make it happen!

Choosing Appropriate Equipment and Containers for Increased Capacity

AS YOU BEGIN the process of scaling up your worm composting, selecting the right equipment and containers is crucial for success. Ensure that your containers are well-ventilated and made of materials suitable for worm habitats. Consider investing in stackable bins or flow-through systems that make harvesting compost a breeze. Let's explore the options and find what suits your needs best.

Strategies for Managing Larger Quantities of Organic Waste and Worms

WITH INCREASED CAPACITY, you'll need to handle larger amounts of organic waste and, of course, take care of more worms. Efficient waste management and maintaining a thriving worm population are essential. We'll provide you with practical tips on feeding schedules, managing moisture levels, and creating a balanced environment. Learn the secrets to keeping your worm army happy and productive!

Handling Potential Problems and Troubleshooting

. . .

SCALING up may come with its fair share of challenges, and being prepared is key to success. We'll address common issues like odor control, pest management, and temperature regulation. Armed with this knowledge, you'll be equipped to tackle any problem that may arise and keep your composting operation running smoothly.

YOU'VE TAKEN a significant step towards becoming a worm composting pro, embracing a small-scale system to a larger-scale success. By carefully choosing the right equipment, managing organic waste and worms efficiently, and tackling potential problems head-on, you're on the path to making a positive impact on the environment while enjoying the rewards of nutrient-rich vermicompost. Keep exploring, experimenting, and learning as you continue your eco-friendly adventure.

Maximizing Compost Production: Organizing and Optimizing Multiple Vermicomposting Systems

TURN kitchen scraps and garden waste into nutrient-rich compost with the help of our wiggly friends, earthworms. In this guide, we'll explore the art of managing multiple compost bins, taking your composting game to a whole new level. By understanding and implementing the strategies we'll discuss, you'll not only save organic matter from ending up in landfills but also create a continuous supply of compost to enrich your garden soil. Let's dive in and discover how to efficiently coordinate and maintain multiple compost bins for maximum compost production.

Organizing Your Composting Space

ASSESS AVAILABLE SPACE and resources for setting up multiple compost bins. Choose an appropriate location that provides proper aeration and protection from extreme weather. Label and map each bin to keep track of its contents and composting stage. Ensure easy access and pathways to facilitate efficient feeding and harvesting.

Implementing Rotation and Maintenance Schedules

ESTABLISH a rotation system to distribute composting loads among bins. Create a maintenance schedule to monitor each bin's progress and address any issues promptly. Regularly turn the compost to promote aeration and accelerate decomposition. Keep a balance between green (nitrogen-rich) and brown (carbon-rich) materials to optimize compost quality.

Coordinating Feeding and Harvesting

SET up a feeding schedule to avoid overloading individual bins. Distribute kitchen scraps and garden waste evenly among the compost bins. Harmonize feeding and harvesting cycles to ensure a constant supply of compost. Use mature compost from one bin to kickstart the process in another, creating a seamless flow of compost production.

Troubleshooting Common Issues

MONITOR compost temperature and moisture levels to avoid potential problems. Address pest infestations with natural solutions to maintain a healthy composting environment. Adjust composting ratios if you encounter foul odors or slow decomposition. Keep an eye out for signs of nutrient deficiencies in the compost and adjust feedstock accordingly.

Engaging with Your Composting

REFLECT on your composting progress and celebrate the milestones achieved. Share your composting success with friends and family to inspire others to join the green movement. Continuously educate yourself about composting techniques and sustainable practices. Embrace composting as a way to connect with nature and make a positive impact on the environment.

YOU'VE COMPLETED MANAGING multiple compost bins and have unlocked the secrets to efficient compost production. By organizing your composting space, implementing rotation and maintenance schedules, and coordinating feeding and harvesting, you've set yourself up for composting success. Remember to troubleshoot common issues and stay engaged in your composting process, always seeking ways to improve and contribute to a greener world. Now, go forth, multiply your compost bins, and let the power of vermicomposting transform your garden and the planet!

Commercial Applications of Vermicomposting: Maximizing Profits through Vermicomposting Ventures

VENTURE on how you can generate revenue from vermicomposting while making a positive impact on the environment. IThink about a business that not only benefits your bottom line but also contributes to a greener and healthier planet. Let's dive into the secrets of turning organic waste into valuable vermicompost products that find eager buyers in various markets.

Exploring Opportunities for Revenue Generation

TO KICKSTART YOUR VERMICOMPOSTING VENTURE, you must first identify the potential revenue streams available. Vermicompost, a nutrient-rich organic fertilizer, is in high demand among environmentally-conscious consumers and agricultural industries. Beyond vermicompost, there are various related products such as worm castings, worm tea, and worm cocoons that can be monetized. Additionally, consider offering vermicomposting workshops and educational programs to further capitalize on your expertise.

Identifying Target Markets and Customers

UNDERSTANDING your target audience is essential for any successful business. Research potential markets for your vermicompost products, such as local gardeners, farmers, nurseries, and landscapers. Health and eco-conscious consumers seeking organic produce are also prime customers. Moreover, exploring collaborations with municipal waste management companies can create a win-win situation for both parties.

Establishing Partnerships and Effective Marketing

FORGE strategic partnerships with local businesses, community gardens, and farmer's markets to expand your reach. Develop a compelling brand identity that highlights the eco-friendly nature of your products. Utilize social media platforms, local events, and content marketing to create awareness and attract customers. Leveraging influencers and environmental activists can help amplify your message.

Ensuring Quality Production and Packaging

To BUILD A LOYAL CUSTOMER BASE, ensure your vermicompost products are of the highest quality. Implement proper waste management techniques, maintain ideal worm habitat conditions, and monitor composting processes diligently. Emphasize sustainability in your packaging, using biodegradable materials to align with your eco-friendly image.

Scaling Up and Diversifying Product Offerings

As YOUR VERMICOMPOSTING business gains momentum, explore opportunities for expansion. Consider vertical integration by growing your own organic crops using your vermicompost. Explore the possibility of breeding and selling worms and cocoons to other vermicomposters. Diversifying your product offerings can safeguard against market fluctuations and increase overall profitability.

Addressing Challenges and Mitigating Risks

No VENTURE IS without its challenges. Understand potential obstacles like fluctuating demand, waste contamination, or adverse weather conditions. Develop contingency plans to mitigate risks and safeguard your business. Stay updated with advancements in vermicomposting technology and adopt innovative practices to stay ahead of the competition.

By now, you understand the immense potential for generating revenue while contributing to a more sustainable planet. Remember, successful vermicomposting ventures require dedication, innovation, and a commitment to quality. Embrace the opportunities, stay informed, and let your passion for environmental sustainability drive your business forward.

unleashing the worm whisperer within

. . .

Advanced Techniques in Vermicomposting

AH, vermicomposting! The delightful dance between worms and waste, turning garbage into gold! You've likely heard of composting, but this isn't your grandma's compost heap. No, my fellow compost enthusiasts, vermicomposting is the hipster cousin of the composting world, using earthworms to create rich, nutrient-packed humus that'll make your plants jump for joy and your soul sing with eco-conscious delight.

Now, before you dismiss this as just another trendy green movement, let me assure you: vermicomposting is not just for the Birkenstock-wearing, kombucha-sipping crowd. No, my friends, it's for everyone who cares about the planet and wants to make a real impact without smelling like a dumpster. It's a game-changer for eco-conscious gardeners, urban farmers, and even apartment dwellers who dare to dream of a mini-garden oasis on their balcony.

A SWARM OF WRIGGLING, happy earthworms feasting on your kitchen scraps, like a foodie frenzy at a gourmet buffet. Their diligent digestion churns out nutrient-rich castings, a black gold so valuable that your plants will sprout rainbows! Sipping your morning coffee while knowing that yesterday's banana peel is busy creating the greenest, most luscious paradise right on your doorstep. Vermicomposting gives you the power to be both the chef and the farm-to-table connoisseur of your garden's dreams.

Now, let's ditch the basics and level up your vermicomposting game with some advanced techniques that'll have you commanding an army of worms like the compost guru you were destined to be:

WORM CHARISMA - Ever felt like you could use some human charm school? Well, move over because it's time to attend Worm Charisma 101. Develop a connection with your worms and channel your inner earthworm whisperer. They may not wag their tails, but they'll wiggle their appreciation for your tender loving care!

THE BISTRO EXPERIENCE - REMEMBER, it's not just about what you feed your worms; it's about how you serve it. Think of it as a fine dining experience for our wriggly friends. Chop, blend, and prep those kitchen scraps, and your worms will thank you with a symphony of healthy castings.

HIGH-RISE LIVING - WHO said worms can't live in luxury? Up your game with a multi-level worm condo. The penthouse floor gets fresh scraps, while the lower levels become worm Utopia, packed with the finest castings fit for a plant king or queen.

THE ART of Breeding - Become the matchmaker of the compost world and encourage your worms to breed like rabbits. More worms mean more compost, and more compost means happier plants and a greener conscience. It's a win-win-win situation!

. . .

WORM FASHIONISTA - WORMS like to feel cozy, too. Dress them in a bed of shredded newspaper, cozy coconut coir, or the finest burlap. After all, a happy worm is a productive worm.

VERMICOMPOSTING Ninja - Time to ninja your composting process! Get stealthy with those compost pests. Introduce beneficial nematodes and predatory mites to keep the bad bugs at bay, while your worms feast like compost kings and queens.

THE WORM ECOSYSTEM - Embrace the concept of harmony and balance by creating a diverse ecosystem in your compost bin. Add a dash of beneficial microbes, a sprinkle of fungi, and a pinch of soil to create the ultimate composting orchestra.

AS MARK TWAIN ONCE SAID, "The secret of getting ahead is getting started." So why not start your vermicomposting adventure today? It's an experience that will transform you from a mere gardener into a compost wizard, harnessing the power of nature's tiniest heroes to make a lasting impact on the planet.

REMEMBER, vermicomposting isn't just a buzzword or a passing fad. It's a practical and empowering way for all of us to take charge of our waste, cultivate our green spaces, and nourish both the earth and our souls. So, embrace the worms, dance with the compost, and let the magic of vermicomposting begin!

Unlocking the Power of Vermicompost Tea: A Guide to Production and Extraction

THE WONDERS of this organic elixir can revolutionize your gardening practices. By the end of this guide, you'll grasp the benefits and applications of vermicompost tea, master the brewing techniques, and gain insights into its optimal use for your plants' health and vitality.

Benefits and Uses of Vermicompost Tea

VERMICOMPOST TEA IS a nutrient-rich liquid extract derived from the breakdown of organic matter by earthworms. By incorporating it into your gardening routine, you'll witness enhanced plant growth, increased resistance to pests and diseases, and improved soil health. This step will illuminate the reasons behind its popularity among eco-conscious gardeners.

Brewing and Extracting Nutrients

GET ready to embark on a brewing adventure! We'll walk you through the process of making vermicompost tea, from selecting the right compost and vermicompost to preparing the brewing equipment. Whether you choose a simple passive method or an aerated approach, we'll guide you every step of the way.

Application Methods and Considerations

APPLYING vermicompost tea is a crucial skill to ensure its efficacy. We'll dive into various application techniques, including foliar spraying and root drenching, empowering you to make the best choices for your plants. Moreover, we'll highlight factors like temperature, storage, and safety precautions to optimize your vermicompost tea application.

. . .

As we explore the world of vermicompost tea, we'll back our claims with trusted sources and scientific research. This way, you can confidently embrace this organic solution, knowing it's rooted in sound knowledge.

Ever wondered how to achieve lush greenery without harmful chemicals? Get ready for a greener, more sustainable gardening experience as we unveil the wonders of vermicompost tea. Ready to join the eco-friendly gardening revolution?

As we wrap up this chapter on vermicompost tea, we hope you've gained valuable insights into its power and potential. With its myriad benefits, brewing techniques, and application methods, vermicompost tea is an eco-friendly game-changer for your garden. Embrace this organic elixir, and witness your plants thrive like never before.

Remember, this is just one chapter of our comprehensive guide to eco-friendly gardening. In the next sections, we'll continue exploring more fascinating topics for the eco-conscious gardener in you. Stay tuned for more insightful wisdom on sustainable practices and the secrets of a thriving garden.

Harnessing Earth's Wonders: Vermiculture for Clean Soil

If you've ever wondered how earthworms and compost can work wonders on contaminated soil, you're about to uncover a groundbreaking solution. In this section, we'll explore the techniques, case studies, and successful projects that demonstrate the power of utilizing vermicomposting for cleaning up polluted environments. By the end, you'll not only understand the science behind it but also gain practical insights into implementing this eco-friendly approach.

Understanding Vermicomposting and Bioremediation

EXPLORE the basics of vermicomposting and how earthworms transform organic waste into nutrient-rich compost. Discover the concept of bioremediation and how it utilizes microorganisms to break down pollutants in the soil.

Techniques for Effective Bioremediation

UNCOVER the specific techniques used in vermicomposting to remediate various types of contaminants. Learn about the importance of temperature, moisture, and aeration in optimizing the bioremediation process.

Case Studies of Successful Bioremediation Projects

GO into real-life success stories of vermicomposting used for cleaning up contaminated sites. Understand the key factors that led to the triumph of these projects and how they can inspire future endeavors.

Practical Advice and Potential Problems

As YOU GO through on your own vermicomposting, keep these insights in mind:

- Use high-quality compost and ensure it's free from potential contaminants to avoid exacerbating the issue.
- Monitor the moisture levels in the compost, as both excessive dryness and extreme dampness can hinder the process.
- Be patient; bioremediation is not an overnight fix, but a sustainable and effective approach that takes time.

By NOW, you've uncovered the wonders of vermicomposting and its potential for bioremediation. With every project, big or small, we can make a significant impact on our environment. So let's roll up our sleeves and start harnessing the power of earth's natural cleaners – the humble earthworms – to transform polluted soil into fertile ground once more.

REMEMBER, it's not just about cleaning up contamination; it's about nurturing a sustainable relationship with nature. As we bid farewell, take these valuable insights with you and let them guide you on your vermicomposting adventure. Together, we can create a world where soil remediation is not just a challenge but an opportunity to reconnect with our planet's astonishing resilience.

Unleashing the Power of Vermicomposting: Exploring Innovative Applications

THE CUTTING-EDGE USED in vermicomposting in diverse fields unlocks the potential of this eco-friendly waste management solution. By understanding and implementing these ground-breaking applications, you'll not only contribute to a sustainable future but also enjoy numerous benefits for yourself and your community.

Vermicomposting in Agriculture and Horticulture

VERMICOMPOST IS a game-changer for farmers and gardeners alike. Earthworms break down organic matter, releasing nutrients in plant-available forms. This natural fertilizer enriches the soil, improving water retention and root development. By incorporating vermicompost, you can boost crop yields, reduce the need for chemical fertilizers, and promote sustainable agriculture.

Vermicomposting in Waste Management

URBAN CENTERS FACE the challenge of managing organic waste efficiently. Vermicomposting offers a low-cost, eco-friendly solution. Worms efficiently process food scraps and green waste, converting them into nutrient-rich compost. Large-scale vermiculture facilities can handle tons of organic waste, diverting it from landfills and closing the loop on food waste.

Vermicomposting in Bioremediation

EARTHWORMS HAVE remarkable abilities to break down organic contaminants, making them valuable allies in bioremediation. In polluted environments, worms consume toxic substances and convert them into harmless compounds, aiding in soil restoration and reducing environmental hazards.

. . .

Vermicomposting in Pharmaceuticals and Medicine

BEYOND AGRICULTURE, vermicompost has potential applications in medicine. Some studies suggest that vermicompost extracts may have medicinal properties, with promising avenues in the pharmaceutical industry. Researchers are investigating the potential health benefits of vermicompost and its role in cultivating medicinal plants.

HAVE you ever wondered how a small worm can turn your kitchen scraps into gold for your garden? Picture a city where organic waste is no longer a burden but a valuable resource nurturing urban green spaces.

YOU CAN NOW EXPLORE the possibilities of harnessing the power of earthworms to transform industries and promote sustainability. Embrace vermicomposting, and join the movement towards a greener, healthier future! The potential is limitless, and it's up to us to make a difference through this remarkable natural process.

vermicomposting for green revolutionaries

. . .

Turning Trash into Treasure

A PLACE FILLED with mountains of waste and shrinking resources, one group of eco-enthusiasts is shaking up the status quo, and they're not afraid to get their hands dirty—literally. Meet the vermicomposters, the guerrilla gardeners, the green revolutionaries of the 21st century, armed with a powerful secret weapon: the humble earthworm.

YOU MIGHT THINK vermiculture is only for granola-crunching tree-huggers or pot-smoking backyard gardeners, but think again. The benefits of vermicomposting reach far beyond just creating a rich, black, and odor-free fertilizer for your precious tomato plants. It's a whole new level of sustainable living and a chance to stick it to the corporate-run world of wastefulness and pollution. So, whether you're an 18-year-old idealist or a seasoned 35-year-old sustainability warrior, get ready to discover the transformative potential of vermicomposting for specific purposes.

"BUT WAIT," you say, "aren't worms just those creepy-crawlies I accidentally step on after a rainy day?" Well, yes, but they're also the unsung heroes of the composting world. A group of underground waste warriors munching their way through your kitchen scraps and turning them into the most nutrient-dense, plant-loving compost you've ever seen. It's like magic, only better—it's science!

WHO SAID composting has to be boring? Sure, you can use your worm castings to grow luscious, organic veggies and impress your friends with your homegrown greens. But why stop there? Vermicomposting has become the latest hipster trend. Hosting a dinner party where you serve food grown in your own worm-powered compost, with a side of "yeah, I'm saving the planet while I'm at it."

ALRIGHT, you're intrigued. But how do you get started on this eco-venture? Fear not, dear reader, for the path to vermicomposting enlightenment is a simple one, paved with decomposing kitchen scraps and wiggling worms.

SET up your luxurious worm hotel in a cozy corner of your apartment or backyard. All your worms need is a spacious bin filled with bedding material (shredded newspaper or cardboard) and a bit of moisture to keep them comfy and content.

SPOIL YOUR WORMS with a gourmet menu of kitchen scraps—fruit and veggie peels, coffee grounds, and even shredded eggshells (they need calcium for strong worm bones, too!). Just avoid anything too greasy, salty, or citrusy—worms are discerning eaters, you know.

DON'T BE a distant worm parent. Get to know your wriggly roommates by spending some quality time observing their daily lives. It's like having your own reality show, but without the drama.

. . .

Patience, young grasshopper. In a few months, your worms will have transformed those scraps into black gold—the nutrient-rich worm castings. Simply harvest and bask in the glory of sustainable composting.

"Vermicomposting is not just a trend; it's a way of life," says Dr. Green Thumb, a leading expert in sustainable gardening. "Worms have the potential to revolutionize waste management and transform our urban landscapes into green oases. It's time we give these earth-saving creatures the respect they deserve!"

Vermicomposting is the ultimate act of rebellion against the wasteful ways of our consumerist society. It's a chance for the 18-year-old dreamer and the 35-year-old eco-warrior to unite in a common purpose—to turn trash into treasure and to pave the way for a greener, more sustainable future. So, grab your compost bin, befriend some worms, and join the ranks of the vermicomposting revolutionaries. Together, we can create a world where sustainability reigns supreme, and the power of worms is celebrated far and wide. Because let's face it, earthworms are the ultimate rockstars of the composting world!

cultivating the green
revolution

. . .

IF THERE'S one undeniable truth in our modern world, it's this: We need to rethink our relationship with waste and embrace more sustainable practices. Enter the Worm Composting Movement, an underground revolution that's anything but slimy or creepy-crawly. It's time to don your green superhero cape, grab a shovel, and join the ranks of the composting warriors!

INSTEAD OF MINDLESSLY TOSSING YOUR kitchen scraps into the trash, they magically transform into nutrient-rich soil, fostering new life and sustaining our planet. Yeah, you heard that right – your veggie peels and coffee grounds become superfood for your garden! Worm composting, or vermicomposting, is the eco-warrior's ultimate secret weapon in the fight against waste and the climate crisis.

STILL SKEPTICAL ABOUT the power of our little wiggle-waggling comrades? Don't be fooled by their size; these wrigglers are the ultimate champions of waste transformation. Let's dive into the worm composting world and explore how you – yes, YOU – can make a real difference in the global fight against waste and climate change.

. . .

WORM COMPOSTING IS NO LONGER a quirky hobby reserved for nature enthusiasts. It's a movement with the potential to transform our environment for the better. This simple, yet profound, practice is about to revolutionize the way we think about waste.

SUSTAINABLE, low-cost, and space-efficient – worm composting is the ideal eco-hack for urban dwellers and young environmentalists. No sprawling backyard required; a small corner in your apartment or balcony will do the trick! Say goodbye to those piles of discarded food packaging – your worms have got your back!

WORMS MIGHT NOT WEAR CAPES, but they possess superpowers that rival any Marvel character. They munch through organic waste like it's their favorite all-you-can-eat buffet, breaking it down into nutrient-packed castings. These castings enrich the soil, boost plant growth, and increase soil water retention. Move over, chemical fertilizers; nature's miracle workers are in town!

OKAY, okay – we get it. The thought of dealing with worms can be intimidating, but fear not! Worms are your composting allies, not foes. They're more reliable than your internet connection and easier to handle than your love life – trust us on that one!

LET'S BE REAL; composting isn't the sexiest topic on social media. But hold up – when you choose worm composting, you're not just being a tree-hugger; you're reducing your carbon buttprint! Landfills emit methane, a potent greenhouse gas, but composting cuts down on those emissions. You'll be turning trash into treasure, all while curbing climate change like a boss.

THIS AIN'T your grandma's compost heap! Worm composting is for everyone who gives a damn about the environment, no matter your age, background, or Instagram followers count. Join the composting revolution, and you'll become an environmental superhero in the eyes of Mother Nature herself.

WORM COMPOSTING ISN'T JUST about feeding your wiggly workforce; it's a transformative process. As you witness your waste turning into black gold, you'll start questioning other aspects of your life. The feedback loop of change kicks in, and soon you'll be reevaluating other choices – from single-use plastics to energy consumption. A small composting bin, a giant leap for sustainable mankind!

REMEMBER, it's not about being perfect or achieving zero waste overnight. Worm composting is a stepping stone towards a greener, more sustainable lifestyle. So, grab a handful of worms, dive into the composting adventure, and become an agent of change in this glorious green revolution! The planet needs you, and your worms are ready to lead the charge!

Vermicomposting: Inspiring Others to Embrace the Worm-Powered Revolution

INSPIRE others to join the vermicomposting revolution. Contributing to a healthier environment, reducing waste, and creating rich soil for your plants – all while engaging in a fascinating and rewarding hobby. Whether you're a seasoned vermicomposter looking to spread the word or a newcomer eager to inspire your community, this guide will equip you with the strategies and knowledge to make a positive impact.

Promoting the Benefits and Importance of Worm Composting

. . .

- **Start with the "Why":** Let's dive right into it! To inspire others, you must first understand and communicate the benefits of vermicomposting. Share how it enriches soil, reduces methane emissions from landfills, and conserves water. Connect with your audience on a personal level, highlighting the positive impact they can have on their own communities.
- **Embrace Visual Storytelling:** A picture is worth a thousand words! Utilize visual aids like infographics, videos, and success stories to captivate your audience. Show them the transformative power of worm composting and its potential to change the world, one bin at a time.

Educational strategies for raising awareness in the community

- **Engage Locally:** Get involved in community events and local gatherings. Host workshops, presentations, or demonstrations on vermicomposting. Engaging with people face-to-face creates a more profound impact and builds a sense of camaraderie among aspiring vermicomposters.
- **Collaborate and Network:** Two heads are better than one, and many hands make light work. Collaborate with gardening clubs, environmental organizations, or schools to spread the word about worm composting. Together, we can amplify our voices and inspire a broader audience.

**Engaging and empowering others to start their own
vermicomposting journey**

- **The "Getting Started" Guide:** Empower others
  with a simple step-by-step guide on setting up their
  vermicomposting system. Include the essentials:
  choosing the right worms, selecting a suitable
  container, and maintaining the composting process.
  Ensure your explanations are clear and concise,
  leaving no room for confusion.
- **Addressing Common Concerns:** People might
  have doubts or fears about starting their
  vermicomposting process. Address these concerns and
  offer practical solutions. Explain the potential
  problems, such as odor or pest issues, and provide
  effective strategies to overcome them.

YOU'VE NOW BECOME A VERMICOMPOSTING ambassador, equipped
with the knowledge to inspire and engage others on this eco-
conscious path. By promoting the benefits, embracing educational strategies, and empowering others to begin vermicomposting, you're actively contributing to a greener, more sustainable
world.

REMEMBER, it all starts with you taking action and sharing your
passion for vermicomposting. As more individuals join this movement, we can collectively make a significant impact on our environment. So, go forth, spread the word, and let the magic of
worm composting inspire change! Together, we can make the
world a better place, one wriggly worm at a time. Happy vermicomposting!

Earthworms Unite: Cultivating Networks & Communities of Vermicomposting Enthusiasts

OUR NATURE'S small but mighty creatures, earthworms, play a starring role in creating nutrient-rich compost for our gardens and plants. In this chapter, we'll explore the power of collaboration among vermicomposters, how it fosters a sense of community, and the benefits of sharing knowledge, experiences, and resources with like-minded individuals.

Why Collaborate in Vermicomposting?

WHEN YOU COLLABORATE with fellow vermicomposters, you open doors to a wealth of opportunities. You'll expand your understanding of vermicomposting, learn new techniques, and even discover innovative ways to overcome challenges. The best part is that you won't be alone on the process; you'll be part of a supportive network of enthusiasts working towards a common goal.

Building Your Vermicomposting Network

START by seeking out local vermicomposting clubs or gardening communities. Attend workshops, seminars, or virtual events focused on composting and sustainable practices. Social media platforms and online forums are also excellent places to connect with fellow vermicomposters from around the world.

Sharing Knowledge and Experiences

. . .

ONCE YOU'VE FOUND your vermicomposting community, don't be shy to share your knowledge and experiences. Each vermicomposter has a unique adventure, and your insights could spark new ideas for others or offer solutions to common challenges. Share your successes, but don't forget to talk about your failures too; these are valuable learning opportunities for everyone.

The Joy of Collaborative Projects

COLLABORATIVE PROJECTS and initiatives in vermicomposting can take your passion to the next level. Working together with your vermicomposting friends on a community composting project or establishing a vermicomposting system in a local school or garden. These endeavors not only enrich the environment but also strengthen the bonds within the vermicomposting community.

Overcoming Challenges Together

As YOU COLLABORATE with fellow vermicomposters, you'll likely encounter various challenges along the way. But remember, you're not alone. Share your difficulties and seek advice from others who may have faced similar issues. Together, you can troubleshoot problems and discover innovative solutions that you might not have considered on your own.

COLLABORATING with fellow vermicomposters is a powerful way to enhance your vermicomposting experience. You'll build a network of like-minded individuals, exchange knowledge, embark on exciting projects, and face challenges head-on as a united force. So, take the first step today – join a vermicomposting community, share your experiences, and sow the seeds of collaboration in this green and sustainable world we are all striving to create.

Growing the Worm Composting Movement: How to Utilize Social Media for Advocacy

SOCIAL MEDIA AS A TOOL EDUCATES, inspires, and mobilizes a community passionate about composting with worms. Whether you're an experienced worm enthusiast or a newbie, harnessing the potential of social media can take your advocacy efforts to new heights. Let's dive in and discover how you can leverage these platforms to make a real difference in promoting sustainable practices.

Utilizing Social Media Platforms for Advocacy

LET'S explore the diverse range of social media platforms at your disposal. From Facebook to Instagram, Twitter to TikTok, each platform offers unique opportunities to connect with like-minded individuals. We'll look into the strengths of each platform and how you can tailor your content to maximize engagement.

Creating Compelling Content with Impact

CONTENT IS king in the realm of social media advocacy. We'll guide you through the art of crafting captivating posts that resonate with your audience. Discover the power of visual storytelling, the impact of video content, and the significance of relatable messaging. Let's ensure your advocacy efforts stand out in the sea of online information.

Engaging with Your Community

BUILDING a vibrant community is essential for any advocacy movement. In this step, we'll discuss strategies to foster meaningful interactions with your followers. Learn how to respond to comments, ask questions, and encourage discussions that promote the growth of your worm composting movement.

Harnessing the Influence of Online Communities

COLLABORATION IS the key to expanding your advocacy reach. We'll explore how to identify and engage with other online communities that share similar environmental interests. By partnering with like-minded groups, you can amplify your message and inspire even more people to join your cause.

EVER WONDERED how to ignite curiosity and spark conversations online? We'll address common experiences and concerns, encouraging you to reflect on your advocacy. What challenges have you faced? What successes have you achieved? Let's engage together and create a supportive environment for sustainable change.

As WE APPROACH the end of our guide, remember that you have the power to make a difference. By harnessing the potential of social media, you can drive the worm composting movement forward and inspire positive environmental change. Embrace the opportunities, connect with your audience, and watch your advocacy efforts bloom.

As you embark on this venture, know that together, we can create a greener, more sustainable world. Thank you for joining us in this mission to grow the worm composting movement and advocate for a better future. Let's compost with worms and sow the seeds of change across the digital landscape!

conclusion

. . .

SUSTAINABILITY IS A PRESSING CONCERN, one simple yet powerful practice has emerged as a beacon of hope for our planet: worm composting. As we've unraveled the fascinating realms of DIY vermiculture, waste management, compost bins, earthworm care, and soil enrichment, we've unlocked a wealth of knowledge that holds the key to transforming our waste into gold – quite literally! From the depths of soil health to the boundless potential of vermicompost, we've unearthed a treasure trove of possibilities that can revolutionize the way we manage organic waste and nourish our ecosystems.

THINK about a place where every individual, from the seasoned gardener to the urban dweller with a tiny balcony, can play a part in promoting a circular economy. A world where we don't see waste as a burden but as a resource to cultivate life, thanks to our tiny, wriggly allies – earthworms. The adventure we've taken together has been a delightful exploration of the interconnectedness of life and how, through conscious choices, we can make a positive impact on our environment.

. . .

FROM OUR FIRST steps into the realm of worm composting, we dived into the depths of understanding the environmental impact of organic waste. Together, we uncovered the multitude of benefits that come with composting alongside these humble creatures. We explored the magical transformation of waste into rich, nutrient-dense vermicompost and witnessed how it can breathe new life into our gardens and farms.

GETTING to know earthworms on a more personal level illuminated their essential role in maintaining soil health. Differentiating between composting and earthworm species opened our eyes to the diverse world of these soil superheroes. We marveled at their intricate anatomy and behavior, realizing just how integral they are to the circle of life.

BUT IT WASN'T all about the worms; we, too, played our part in creating a harmonious vermicomposting system. Together, we rolled up our sleeves and learned how to select the perfect location, choose the right compost bin, and create a nurturing environment for our earthworm allies. As we saw our composting setup come to life, we couldn't help but feel a sense of pride and wonder.

WITH OUR VERMICOMPOSTING SYSTEM THRIVING, we turned our attention to caring for our earthworm friends. Moisture levels, temperature control, and pest management all became essential factors in maintaining a happy and healthy worm community. As we troubleshooted and problem-solved, we grew more adept at nurturing this fragile balance.

THE HIGHLIGHT of our process was undoubtedly witnessing the transformation of organic waste into vermicompost gold. From understanding the best materials to compost to mastering the art of composting food scraps, we embraced the magic of this natural alchemy. Our vermicompost grew into a precious resource that could revitalize any garden or farm, and we felt a renewed sense of purpose in becoming stewards of the earth.

As we scaled up our vermiculture operation, we uncovered the potential for entrepreneurship and commercial applications. The possibilities for generating revenue from vermicomposting and connecting with like-minded individuals expanded our vision beyond our gardens. We envisioned a world where the worm composting movement thrives, where individuals come together to educate and inspire others to embark on this transformative experience.

And so, our story unfolds, chapter by chapter, revealing the beauty and simplicity of worm composting made easy. No longer burdened by waste, we've embraced a symbiotic relationship with nature, where we give back as much as we take. The lessons learned, the laughter shared, and the joy of creating a greener, more sustainable world have filled our hearts with hope and determination.

As we bid farewell to this chapter of our tale, we take with us the knowledge that each one of us can be an agent of positive change. No matter how big or small our actions may seem, they can ripple outward and make a profound impact on our planet. Worm composting isn't just about enriching our soil; it's about cultivating a deeper connection with nature and with one another.

So let's continue this hand in hand with our earthworm allies, inspiring and empowering others to embrace the transformative power of worm composting. Let's build communities that share knowledge, experience, and resources, fostering a sustainable movement that spans far beyond the pages of this book.

. . .

As WE PART WAYS, know that you hold the keys to a brighter, greener future. Go forth and share your vermicomposting wisdom, tell your friends, and spread the word. Our world needs more vermicomposters – individuals who dare to dream of a planet where waste becomes nourishment and where life blooms in abundance.

If you enjoyed this book please leave a review so others can find it and benefit they way we hope you have!

AVAILABLE NOW AT **LIFELEVELUPBOOKS.COM**

1. **First Time Gardening Advice:** The Beginner's Journey Into Successful Gardening - Discover the Joy and Satisfaction of Growing Your Own Garden
2. **Organic Vegetable Gardening at Home:** Sustainable Planning, Soil Preparation, Seed Selection, Pest Control, and Harvesting
3. **Make Money Growing Microgreens:** A Step-By-Step Book to Earn Passive Income From Your Indoor Garden: Growing, Marketing, and Selling Microgreens for a Sustainable Business
4. **Aquaponics for Homeowners:** Setup, Water Quality, Plant and Fish Selection, System Maintenance, and Organic Food Production
5. **Worm Composting Made Easy:** DIY Vermiculture, Waste Management, Compost Bins, Earthworm Care, and Soil Enrichment

Made in United States
North Haven, CT
09 June 2024

53414262R00063